Chinese Feasts & Festivals

A Cookbook

Chinese Feasts & Festivals

A COOKBOOK

recipes & illustrations by
S.C. Moey

PERIPLUS

For mom…

Published by Periplus Editions, with editorial offices at 130 Joo Seng Road #06-01, Singapore 368357.
Tel: (65) 6280-1330 Fax: (65) 6280-6290 Email: inquiries@periplus.com.sg Website: www.periplus.com

Distributed by
North America, Latin America and Europe: Tuttle Publishing, 364 Innovation Drive, North Clarendon, VT 05759-9436
Tel: (802) 773-8930 Fax: (802) 773-6993 Email: info@tuttlepublishing.com Website: www.tuttlepublishing.com

Japan: Tuttle Publishing, Yaekari Building, 3rd Floor, 5-4-12 Osaki, Shinagawa-ku, Tokyo 141-0032
Tel: 81 (03) 5437-0171 Fax: 81 (03) 5437-0755 Email: tuttle-sales@gol.com

Asia Pacific: Berkeley Books Pte Ltd, 130 Joo Seng Road #06-01, Singapore 368357
Tel: (65) 6280-1330 Fax: (65) 6280-6290 Email: inquiries@periplus.com.sg Website: www.periplus.com

10 09 08 07 06
5 4 3 2

Contents

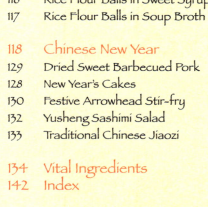

Author's Preface

It is often said that the Chinese live to eat. Happily for them, China's rich history and culture have, with heaven's mandate, conspired to fill the traditional calendar with a generous round of festivities at which all their gastronomic longings can be fulfilled.

One good turn deserves another. To honor the benevolent powers that make all things possible, the Chinese install in their homes various guardians — some people call them gods — who at the appropriate times are invited to participate in human festivities and are plied with food and drink. The gods eat the spiritual essence of the offerings and man consumes the delectable substance. Chinese ancestors, who are considered on a par with the gods, are revered and worshiped in the same way with a glorious repast.

Cooking for both man and the gods is thus an event rich in symbolism — bringing wealth, happiness, luck and prosperity — all the things that man desires and which the gods can provide. Cooking for important festive occasions like this may seem like a formidable task, and certainly in the old days it was an enormous job, though nobody minded or even noticed. Fowls had to be plucked. Shark's fins, sea cucumbers, bamboo shoots, to name just a few of the ingredients, needed to be soaked, cleaned, boiled and re-boiled — processes that could take several days. There were no short cuts, no labor-saving devices, and everything had to also be cooked over charcoal fires. For most cooks today, these would present insurmountable obstacles. Fortunately, time has taken much of the hard work out of cooking. Today, it is possible to cook for feasts and festivals without breaking one's back. It can be quite an enjoyable exercise, in fact, thanks to refrigeration, the wide range of modern kitchen appliances available, and the presence of supermarkets stocked with ready-to-use ingredients.

I am privileged to come from a family whose ways are steeped in tradition, and to live in a community which takes great pride in the vibrant expression of its culture. From this great storehouse of knowledge and experience, I have been able to assemble a few culinary facts and fancies, as well as a collection of recipes for the Chinese food lover to read and enjoy or, if the spirit takes flight, to use in cooking up a feast that will impress the ancestors, win approval from the gods, and certainly please the family as well as friends.

S.C.Moey
Penang, 2005

PART ONE

The Chinese Feast

For food to be a truly joyous experience, there must be appropriate occasions to eat, drink and make merry. The Chinese are not short of such occasions. For more than 2,000 years, tradition has satisfied their desire to celebrate through a plethora of festivals, reunions, weddings and anniversaries.

Chinese festival feasts are purely family affairs. Gods and ancestors are invited to the party, but otherwise "outsiders" are generally excluded. The food served on these occasions is a combination of symbols and sumptuous flavors, a spiritual celebration and an earthly pleasure. Dishes suggesting wealth, luck and splendor by way of their appearance or because they rhyme with certain auspicious Chinese words, simmer or saute in pots and woks. Proportions are generous as custom dictates that one should not stint at the festive table. Abundance brings luck. For families of modest means, surplus is restricted to these special occasions. Hence festivals, with their promise of cornucopia, are eagerly awaited.

Before man can enjoy, the gods must be nourished. In Chinese homes, gods and ancestors take the form of tablets — red wooden or metal rectangles mounted on the wall, fitted with jars or cylinders for candles and joss sticks. Calligraphic characters in black or gold identify the ancestors. Three "protectors" — the Heavenly Emperor or Jade Emperor, the Earth God and the Kitchen God — are installed to look after the home. People in need of "extra protection" reinforce these with additional help from the God of Wealth, the Warrior God (Guan Gong) and the Goddess of Mercy (Kuan Yin). Food and wine are set on a tray or table before each tablet. The most efficacious offerings are chicken, roast pork, fresh lettuce, spring onions, celery, rice, sweet rice cakes and fruits — all symbolic of life and its attendant virtues and values. The same delicacies may be offered to the three household gods, who are worshiped in turns. Extra places are set in case a god has company. Popular imagination assigns two bodyguards to each celestial VIP.

Traditionally, the lady of the house conducts the offering rites. Once the food is set, the protector and his entourage, if any, are welcomed with two red candles. This is followed by an offering of joss sticks together with prayers and, if one desires, divination sticks or blocks are cast to determine the visitors' wishes and receive their blessings. A suitable time is allowed to pass during which the invisible guests eat and drink. The entertainments over, they are given a send-off with a ceremonial burning of an assortment of joss papers (*yim po* in Cantonese) conveying good wishes and a safe journey.

For the ancestors, customarily the last of the protectors to partake of the feast, an even larger spread is laid out. Again, three places are set, though in some households the settings can reach ten or twelve. The family patriarch, proffering joss sticks, leads the way. Other males take precedence over females. Appeased, the ancestors feast in a fashion peculiar to the gods, unseen and undetected by mortals.

Protection is renewed when the divine have departed. Secure in the knowledge, members of the household gather and enjoy the feast they have shared with the gods and the ancestors.

Poultry Recipes

In the old days, it was customary to present gifts of live poultry, the bearer conveying the joy of living things to the recipient and his household. A pair of handsome capons created a stir whenever they were presented. Those were the days when fowl was a luxury.

Times change. Today, this practice had lost its appeal. Indeed, for people used to modern conveniences, a live chicken is considered more a bane than a boon. A battle with a live, squawking bird takes away much of the pleasure of receiving it. Dressing it may even spoil the appetite. But it is also not smart to resort to the dressed, ready-to-cook variety. It may even be risky, considering the special significance attached to the deed. One may not get through the front door bearing a couple of lifeless birds. To be sure, nothing unsettles the superstitious Chinese more than violating customary laws, as to do so is to invite misfortune. So generally today only cooked food or red packets containing money (*hongbao*) are given as gifts on special occasions.

The obligatory offering for the gods is a whole cooked chicken, head propped up, wings and feet neatly tucked into the body, accompanied by strips of roast pork, bunches of fresh green lettuce, stalks of celery and spring onions. The chicken represents the phoenix, the mythical bird that rose from the ashes, symbolizing life after death.

Duck is also a festive favorite, though in Cantonese homes it is not accorded the same status as the chicken, and is not offered whole to the household gods. According to the fastidious Cantonese, a duck's flattened countenance (*pien how, pien mien*: literally "flat mouth, flat face" in Cantonese, an expression people associate with woe) simply does not fit into the celebratory scheme of "all things bright and beautiful" and may only be offered as a dish in which its form is no longer recognizable. Provincial customs differ. In Fukienese households, two whole birds — a duck and a chicken — are required to appease the ancestors. These are boiled, a method used since ancient times. Nowadays, roast duck is also acceptable, or even boiled duck eggs in the case of shrinking households. The chicken, however, persists as a permanent feature in all ceremonial feasts, cooked according to a tradition originating from the north when people offered boiled white meats to the gods of Manchuria.

Homestyle White Chicken

The feast that the Chinese prepare to mark each festival always includes this dish. Boiling is the traditional method, with the stock reserved for soups and sauces. From this basic recipe, a variety of dishes can be created by simply varying the accompanying ingredients and condiments, as is the convention in formal dinners. At home, the chicken is usually served plain with a number of condiments placed in tiny sauce bowls. Soy sauce, oyster sauce, chili sauce and mustard are among the favorite condiments.

2 teaspoons salt
1 fresh chicken, cleaned and dried
1 pip star anise (optional)
3 spring onions, trimmed
3 to 4 slices fresh ginger
1/4 teaspoon sesame oil

CHILI DIPPING SAUCE
6 finger-length red chilies, halved and deseeded
1/4 cup (60 ml) chicken stock (from the boiled chicken)
Pinch of salt

GINGER DIP
1 1/2 in (4 cm) fresh ginger
2 spring onions, finely sliced
1/2 teaspoon salt
1 tablespoon oil

Serves 6 to 8
Preparation time: 30 mins
Cooking time: 25 mins

1 Sprinkle the salt on the chicken and rub well over the entire body including the body cavity. Set aside.

2 Bring a large pot of water (8 cups/2 liters) and all the other ingredients to a boil over high heat. Hold the chicken above the pot by firmly grasping one of its legs with one hand, and then ladle the simmering broth all over the chicken using a soup ladle in the other hand, allowing the broth to pass through the body cavity. Continue to ladle the broth over the chicken until it is lightly scalded all over and changes color, then immerse the whole chicken into the boiling broth, breast side up. Cover and boil the chicken for 15 minutes, then turn off the heat and leave the chicken to steep in the pot for 15 to 20 minutes. Remove the chicken and plunge it immediately into iced water for about 15 minutes to stop the cooking process, then drain thoroughly. Strain and reserve the stock.

3 Make the Chili Dipping Sauce by grinding the chilies to a paste in a mortar or blender. Combine the chili paste, chicken stock and salt, and mix until well blended. Transfer to a serving bowl.

4 Prepare the Ginger Dip by peeling and grating or grinding the ginger, then placing the ground ginger in a small serving dish and topping it with the spring onion and salt. Heat the oil in a skillet until very hot and pour it over the ginger and spring onion. Lightly stir the mixture to blend.

5 Slice the cooked chicken into serving pieces, arrange on a large serving platter and serve with the Chili Dipping Sauce and Ginger Dip.

NOTE: If you prefer, you may steam the chicken instead of boiling it. Place the salted chicken on a steaming tray together with the spring onions and ginger. Fill a large wok a third full with water and bring the water to a boil over high heat. Place a wire rack in the wok and set the dish with the chicken on it. Cover the wok and steam the chicken over rapidly boiling water for about 45 minutes, adding more hot water whenever the water runs low. Alternatively, steam in a steamer.

Drunken Chicken

In this *Sichuanese* recipe, the plain Homestyle White Chicken is transformed into
yet another classic dish by marinating it in fragrant Shao Xing rice wine. Drunken Chicken
makes an excellent starter. At formal dinners and banquets, it is often served as a component
in the elaborately assembled cold dish appetizer platter.

2 spring onions, bruised
   with a cleaver or pestle
3 slices fresh ginger
2 teaspoons salt
1/2 fresh chicken or 3 chicken
   legs, cleaned and dried
1 cup (250 ml) chicken stock
1 cup (250 ml) rice wine
   (preferably Shao Xing)
Few sprigs of coriander leaves
   (cilantro), to garnish

SOY DIP
1 in (2 1/2 cm) fresh ginger
4 tablespoons soy sauce
1/4 cup (60 ml) chicken stock
   (from the steamed chicken)

1 Combine the bruised spring onions, ginger slices and salt in a small
bowl and mix well. Rub the mixture into the chicken, then place it
on a heatproof dish and set aside for 1 hour to allow the flavors to
penetrate. Steam the chicken with the spring onions and ginger slices
on a rack in a covered wok (see page 19) or steamer over high heat for
about 30 minutes until cooked. Turn off the heat and allow the
chicken to cool. Discard the spring onions and ginger, drain the
chicken and reserve the chicken stock, adding some water if necessary
to make 1 cup (250 ml). Alternatively, you may boil the chicken by
following the recipe for Homestyle White Chicken (see page 14),
and use part of it as required for this recipe, reserving 1 cup (250 ml)
of the chicken stock.
2 Slice the chicken into thin pieces and pack them, with the skin
sides facing down, into a deep dish in 2 or 3 layers. Combine the
rice wine and reserved chicken stock in a small bowl and mix well.
Pour the mixture over the chicken pieces, cover the dish with plastic
wrap and refrigerate overnight.
3 Prepare the Soy Dip by first peeling and grating or ginding the
ginger, then combining it with all the ingredients and mixing well.
Transfer to a serving bowl, and provide individual dipping bowls for
diners to help themselves.
4 When the chicken is ready to be served, place a serving platter
over the dish and carefully invert the chicken onto the serving platter,
keeping it neatly layered. Garnish with coriander leaves (cilantro)
and serve cold with the Soy Dip on the side.

Serves 4   Preparation time: 25 mins + overnight chilling   Cooking time: 30 mins

Crispy Fried Chicken

Given the size of Chinese families, it is not unusual to cook more than one chicken dish for large family gatherings. Crispy Fried Chicken is always a favorite because of the delicious crispness of the skin. In this recipe, it is important to dry the chicken thoroughly to get that crispness. Traditionally, the chicken is hung out to dry in the sun for several hours, but the same effect can be achieved using a hair dryer.

1 ½ teaspoons salt
1 fresh chicken, cleaned and dried
Oil for deep-frying
Cucumber slices, to garnish
Bottled sweet chili sauce, for
   dipping (optional)

MARINADE
1 teaspoon honey
2 teaspoons soy sauce
2 tablespoons ginger juice (from
   2 in/5 cm freshly grated ginger)
Pinch of freshly ground black
   pepper

1 Sprinkle the salt on the chicken and rub well over the entire body including the body cavity. Set aside.

2 Prepare the Marinade by combining all the ingredients in a bowl and mixing well. Pour the Marinade over the chicken and rub it in with your fingers. Leave it to marinate for at least 1 hour, turning the chicken over once or twice or basting it with the Marinade occasionally. The marinated chicken must be drained off all excess liquid and dried before deep-frying. Place the chicken on a rack placed over a bowl, and blow it dry with a hair dryer for 8 to 10 minutes.

3 Heat the oil in a wok over medium heat until very hot. Gently lower the chicken into the hot oil and deep-fry for about 15 minutes on each side, ladling hot oil from the bottom of the wok over the chicken from time to time, until the chicken is golden brown and evenly cooked. Remove and drain on paper towels.

4 Cut the chicken into serving pieces and arrange on a serving platter. Garnish with cucumber slices and serve immediately as it is, or with sweet chili sauce as the dip.

Serves 4 to 6   Preparation time: 40 mins + 1 hour to marinate + 10 mins drying
Cooking time: 30 mins

Baked Stuffed Chicken Wings

In Chinese cuisine, a rose is often known by another name. The chicken becomes a phoenix, a symbol of female power. "Flight of the Phoenix" and "Winged Empress" are two of the fanciful names given to this dish. Having to debone and stuff wings sounds like a lot of trouble, but you can prepare and cook them well in advance. They taste just as good when served cold. Sliced into disks, they make delightful starters.

6 chicken wings

2 chicken breasts (about 10 oz /300 g in total), chilled in the refrigerator for 4 hours, sliced

2 tablespoons soy sauce

1 tablespoon oyster sauce

1 tablespoon fish sauce (*yue lo*)

$^1/_2$ teaspoon sugar

$^1/_4$ teaspoon ground white pepper

2 tablespoons oil

6 lettuce leaves, to garnish

Bottled sweet chili sauce, for dipping

NOTE: You may deep-fry the stuffed wings and they taste just as good. Mix the ground meat with $^1/_2$ teaspoon of cornstarch and season it in the same manner. Stuff the meat into the wings and deep-fry the stuffed wings in hot oil over medium heat for 6 to 8 minutes on each side.

1 Debone each chicken wing by cutting around the bone at the top part of the drummette (the section with a single bone that looks like a mini drumstick) with a paring knife to detach the skin from the bone. Push the skin down to expose the meat. Carefully scrape the meat off the bone and reserve the meat. Twist the bone and rotate it at the joint until it is pulled out. Discard the bone. In the same manner, scrape off the meat and pull out the two bones from the wing blade, without tearing the skin and leaving the wing tip intact. Debone all the chicken wings in this manner.

2 Combine the chicken breast and meat from the chicken wings, and grind to a paste in a food processor. Transfer to a mixing bowl.

3 Preheat the oven to 400°F (200°C).

4 Combine the sauces, sugar and pepper in a small bowl and mix until the sugar is dissolved. Pour half of the sauce mixture over the ground meat and mix until well combined. Divide into 6 equal portions and stuff each deboned wing with a portion of the seasoned meat using a small spoon. Place the stuffed wings on a baking tray.

5 Add the oil to the remaining sauce mixture and mix well. Brush the stuffed wings with the sauce mixture and bake in the oven for about 20 minutes. Remove from the heat.

6 Brown the baked wings under an electric broiler or in the oven for about 5 minutes on each side, basting with the remaining sauce mixture.

7 Serve the stuffed wings whole or cut crosswise into disks. Arrange them on a serving platter lined with a bed of lettuce leaves and serve immediately with a dipping bowl of sweet chili sauce on the side.

Serves 4 to 6   Preparation time: 1 hour   Cooking time: 30 mins

Tea Smoked Duck

Smoked duck is a specialty of Sichuan and Hunan, interior provinces which share many similarities in cooking. Deep-fried smoked duck is delicious. Apart from tea leaves, pine cones or camphor wood can also be used to smoke the bird in the wok the traditional way, or in the oven.

1 ¹/₂ tablespoons salt

1 fresh duck, cleaned and dried

Aluminum foil

5 tablespoons black tea leaves

2 to 3 tablespoons sugar

1 teaspoon sesame oil

Cucumber slices, to garnish

MARINADE

2 tablespoons rice wine

3 spring onions, bruised with a cleaver or pestle

6 slices fresh ginger, bruised with a cleaver or pestle

¹/₂ teaspoon freshly ground black pepper

DIPPING SAUCE

2 tablespoons hot bean sauce

4 tablespoons plum sauce

1 tablespoon soy sauce

¹/₂ teaspoon sesame oil

NOTE: Alternatively, you can smoke the duck in an oven. Spread the tea leaves and sugar mixture in a shallow pan lined with aluminum foil and place the pan on the lowest rack of a preheated oven. Place the duck on the middle rack and bake at very high heat (480°F/250°C) for 8 to 10 minutes, turning the duck over once.

1 Sprinkle the salt on the duck and rub well over the entire body including the body cavity. Set aside.

2 Combine the Marinade ingredients in a small bowl and mix well. Rub the Marinade into the duck and body cavity with your fingers. Allow to marinate for at least 1 hour, turning the duck over once or twice and basting it with the Marinade occasionally. Transfer to a heatproof dish.

3 Combine the Dipping Sauce ingredients in a serving bowl and mix well. Set aside.

4 Fill a large wok a third full with water and bring the water to a boil over high heat. Place a wire or cake rack in the wok and set the dish with the duck on it. Cover the wok and steam the duck over rapidly boiling water for 1 hour until tender, adding more hot water whenever the water runs low. Remove from the heat and set aside to cool. Drain off the sauce and fat, and discard the spring onions and ginger.

5 To smoke the steamed duck, line the bottom of a wok with double layers of aluminum foil. Combine the tea leaves and sugar, and spread the mixture evenly on the foil. Place a wire rack or criss-crossed chopsticks over the tea leaves and carefully balance the duck on top, making sure it does not touch the leaves. Cover the wok and heat over high heat until smoke begins to escape from under the lid, 3 to 5 minutes. Reduce the heat to very low and continue to smoke the duck for another 8 to 10 minutes until golden brown. Turn off the heat and leave the duck in the covered wok for 5 to 10 minutes to brown further. Remove from the wok and lightly brush the whole duck with sesame oil.

6 Cut the duck into bite-sized pieces and arrange on a serving platter. Garnish with cucumber slices and serve immediately with the bowl of Dipping Sauce on the side.

Serves 6 to 8   Preparation time: 25 mins + 1 hour to marinate
Cooking time: 1 hour 15 mins

Fragrant Tender Duck

This all-time Cantonese favorite goes by the Cantonese name *heong so ngap*, meaning "fragrant tender duck" and involves steaming and frying a duck that has been marinated in soy, five spice powder and wine. It is delicious to eat on its own or with Mandarin Pancakes.

2 teaspoons salt
1 fresh duck, cleaned and dried
3 tablespoons cornstarch
Oil for deep-frying
2 spring onions, cut into lengths
Hoisin sauce, for dipping

MARINADE
$\frac{1}{2}$ teaspoon five spice powder
$\frac{1}{2}$ teaspoon freshly ground
black pepper
1 tablespoon soy sauce
1 tablespoon rice wine
Few drops red food coloring
(optional)

MANDARIN PANCAKES
2 cups (300 g) flour, sifted
1 cup (250 ml) boiling water
1 teaspoon sesame oil

NOTE: The pancakes can be prepared up to a day in advance. Before serving, reheat by steaming the pancakes in a wok or steamer, lined with a clean towel, for about 10 minutes. If preferred, you may buy the readymade Chinese Pancakes from the supermarket, instead of making your own for this recipe.

1 Sprinkle the salt on the duck and rub well over the entire body including the body cavity. Set aside.
2 Combine the Marinade ingredients in a bowl and mix well. Rub the Marinade into the duck and body cavity with your fingers. Allow to marinate for at least 1 hour, basting the duck with the Marinade from time to time. Transfer the duck to a heatproof dish.
3 Steam the marinated duck for 1 hour in a covered wok (see page 19) until tender. Remove and set aside to cool.
4 While the duck is steaming, prepare the Mandarin Pancakes. Place the flour in a mixing bowl and make a well in the center. Gradually stir in the boiling water and sesame oil, mixing well with chopsticks or a wooden spoon. Flour your hands and on a lightly floured surface, knead the soft sticky mixture into a smooth dough, about 10 minutes. Cover the dough with a cloth and allow to rest for 30 minutes.
5 Divide the dough into 2 equal portions. Roll each portion into a cylinder, then slice it into 14 to 15 equal pieces. Roll each piece into a small ball between your palms. Flatten each ball slightly with your palm, and using a rolling pin, roll it out into a thin circle, about 4 in (10 cm) in diameter. Place the dough circles on a large tray, covering them with a cloth or plastic wrap to prevent them from drying out. Heat a non-stick pan and dry-fry the pancakes over low heat until small bubbles appear, about 1 minute on each side. Transfer the pancakes to a serving platter.
6 Dredge the steamed duck in the cornstarch until evenly coated. Heat the oil in a wok over medium heat until very hot. Gently lower the coated duck into the hot oil and deep-fry for 5 to 10 minutes on each side, ladling hot oil from the bottom of the wok over the duck from time to time until the duck is golden brown and evenly cooked. Remove from the heat and drain on paper towels.
7 Separate the duck meat from the bone and slice thinly. Arrange on a serving platter and serve with spring onion, pancakes and a dipping bowl of hoisin sauce. Alternatively, cut the duck into serving pieces and serve with steamed rice.

Serves 6 to 8   Preparation time: 45 mins + 1 hour to marinate
Cooking time: 1 hour 30 mins

Steamed Duck with Bamboo Shoots

This is a good dish to serve piping hot with steamed rice. If preferred, other ingredients like leafy greens, Chinese cabbage, dried oysters and chestnuts may be added. You can also try other interesting combinations, such as gingko nuts and water chestnuts. If using ingredients that need long cooking like dried gingko nuts and black Chinese mushrooms, steam these together with the duck instead of adding them at the end.

1 fresh duck

$^1/_2$ teaspoon ground white pepper

1 teaspoon salt

3 tablespoons soy sauce

$^1/_2$ cup (125 ml) oil

8 black Chinese mushrooms, soaked until soft, stems discarded, caps halved

8 dried scallops ($^1/_3$ cup/40 g), soaked for 30 minutes, drained

3 spring onions, trimmed

2 in (5 cm) fresh ginger, peeled and sliced

2 tablespoons rice wine

$^1/_2$ teaspoon sugar (optional)

1 can or 1 packet bamboo shoots (about 7 oz/200 g), thinly sliced to yield about 1 cup

10 snow peas, tops and tails removed

1 teaspoon cornstarch, dissolved in 1 tablespoon water

Sprigs of coriander leaves (cilantro), to garnish

1 Clean the duck and dry it with paper towels, then sit the duck up on its neck, with its legs up and breast side facing you. To split the duck, hold the duck firmly with one hand and use a sharp cleaver or knife with the other hand to cut through the breastbone and downward along the midpoint until the neck. Use your hands to pull the duck apart, then press both sides of the breast downward to flatten them slightly. Rub the pepper and salt into the underside of the duck.

2 Bring a big pot of water to a boil over high heat. Immerse the duck in the boiling water and boil uncovered for about 10 minutes, skimming off the foam and fat that float to the surface. Remove the duck from the pot and drain until dry. Rub 2 tablespoons of the soy sauce over the entire duck. Reserve 2 cups (500 ml) of the stock from the boiled duck.

3 Heat the oil in a large wok over medium heat and fry the duck for 3 to 5 minutes until browned, turning over once. Remove the duck from the pan and drain on paper towels, then tuck in the wings and tuck the legs into the body. Place the duck in a heatproof casserole dish along with the mushroom, dried scallops, spring onions and ginger. Add the rice wine, remaining soy sauce, sugar (if using) and reserved stock. Steam in a large wok (see page 19) or steamer for about 1 $^1/_2$ hours, adding more hot water when the water runs low. Turn off the heat, discard the spring onions and ginger, and transfer the duck to a cutting board. Cut the duck into serving pieces and arrange on a serving platter with the mushroom and scallops.

4 Pour the juices from the duck into a small saucepan. Skim off the excess fat and boil over medium heat until it reduces to about 1 $^1/_2$ cups (375 ml). Add the bamboo shoots and snow peas, and boil for 1 more minute. Reduce the heat to low, stir in the cornstarch mixture and mix until the sauce thickens. Remove from the heat and pour the sauce over the duck pieces. Garnish with coriander leaves and serve hot with steamed rice.

Serves 6 to 8   Preparation time: 30 mins   Cooking time: 1 $^1/_2$ to 2 hours

芋头鸭

Braised Duck with Yellow Bean Paste

Yellow bean paste is similar to Japanese miso — made from salted, fermented soybeans — and it gives a wonderfully rich flavor to this dish. Taro is a large, brown-skinned root which turns slightly purplish on cooking. Taro with duck is an intriguing combination, popularized by the Hainanese.

1 fresh duck

8 to 10 black peppercorns

2 tablespoons yellow bean paste (*tau cheo*)

2 onions, peeled and sliced

4 cloves garlic

1 in (2 ¹/₂ cm) fresh ginger, peeled and sliced

1 tablespoon oil

2 ¹/₂ cups (625 ml) water

1 taro (about 1 lb/500 g), peeled, cut into wedges (optional)

1 teaspoon salt

1 Clean the duck, removing any fatty bits, then dry and cut it into serving pieces.

2 Grind the peppercorns in a peppermill or mortar until fine, then combine with the bean paste, onion, garlic and ginger, and grind to a smooth paste. Transfer to a bowl and set aside.

3 Heat the oil in a wok over medium heat and stir-fry the ground ingredients until fragrant, 3 to 5 minutes. Add the duck pieces and stir-fry for another 3 to 5 minutes. Stir in the water, increase the heat to high and bring the mixture to a boil, then cover and simmer for 1 to 1 ¹/₂ hours. Reduce the heat to medium, add the taro, mix well and simmer covered for about 30 minutes until tender. Finally, season with the salt, remove from the heat and transfer to a serving bowl.

4 As duck releases a large amount of fat during cooking, skim this off from the dish before serving. Serve the dish hot with steamed rice.

Serves 6 to 8   Preparation time: 25 mins   Cooking time: 2 hours

Meat Recipes

For millions of Chinese battling constantly with shortages, meat on the table has always been a sign of better times. When there is a reason to feast, adequate is not nearly good enough. Abundance — if one has the means to afford it — is better, symbolizing luck and good fortune.

In Chinese festival cooking, pork, mutton and beef are all used, but pork is the celebratory meat: the nourishment of gods, favored by man, and coveted by spirits. Whole roast pigs are standard offerings at clan gatherings, weddings and thanksgiving celebrations. According to some provincial customs, they are also obligatory at funerals. When the festivities are over, the meat is carved up and distributed. Friends and relatives in attendance can look forward to taking "a piece of luck" home and sharing it with their families. At home, where such excesses are not possible or even practical during festival times, the gods understandingly exact no more than a modest joint of roast pork as appeasement.

Feasting on roast pigs at weddings and funerals was a custom of the Manchurian people. At such functions, the piece de resistance — a whole cooked pig — was placed on a red carpet on the floor. Guests armed with knives sat around the pig and helped themselves to whichever part took their fancy. When the Manchus ruled China during the Qing Dynasty, imperial approval raised the boar's esteem to new heights. Every day at the imperial palace, two pigs were cooked to venerate the gods. During the Chinese New Year, the emperor himself would present the offerings. When the ceremony was over, the meat was distributed among his retainers. Those who performed well during the year were assured of a portion.

While pork owed much of its popularity to the Qing potentates, mutton was a legacy of the Mongols. Lamb was brought into China by these invaders from the desert interior, the founders of the Yuan Dynasty. But the Chinese soon discovered new ways to cook the meat. It is used in much the same way as beef, treated with ginger and spring onions to transform the strong flavor characteristic of red meats to one of subtlety, much preferred by the Chinese. Pot roasts and stir-fries are popular methods of cooking. Another favorite style is fondue — steamboat or firepot is also used to describe this mode of eating — where thin slices of meat are dipped into boiling stock together with other items, including vegetables. Beef and mutton, however, do not add up to ambrosia. Though regularly served at the festive table, particularly in the northern and interior provinces, they are food for the enjoyment of man and need not be offered to the gods, a sign of their "foreign" origins.

Roast Pork

Although it is not difficult, Chinese housewives rarely prepare roast pork at home, as it is so readily available. Everyone has her favorite roast pork vendor, and he can be found anywhere: in the marketplace or a neighborhood food shop. Frequently, such vendors have a whole roast pig to carve from, to the satisfaction of their customers. Gods take the meat plain but man may need a dash of soy, oyster or hoisin sauce to enhance the meat.

2 ½ lbs (1 kg) pork belly with
   skin left on, cleaned and dried
Sprigs of coriander leaves
   (cilantro), to garnish
Soy sauce, oyster sauce or hoisin
   sauce, to serve

SEASONING A
2 teaspoons five spice powder
1 teaspoon salt
1 clove garlic, finely minced
2 teaspoons minced coriander
   leaves (cilantro)
½ teaspoon sugar

SEASONING B
1 teaspoon salt
1 tablespoon vinegar

1 Place the pork on a flat surface with the skin side down and using a fine needle, prick the meat all over at close intervals. Combine all the ingredients for *Seasoning A* in a small bowl and mix well, then rub the mixture into the meat. Turn the meat over and using a sharp needle, score the skin by making deep pricks at close intervals. Combine the ingredients for *Seasoning B* in a small bowl and rub the mixture into the skin. Place the pork in a heatproof dish with the skin side up and leave overnight in the refrigerator, uncovered.

2 Preheat the oven to very hot (480°F/250°C).

3 Roast the pork, skin side up, in the oven for 10 minutes. Reduce the heat to 350°F (180°C) and continue roasting for another 50 minutes. Remove the pork from the oven.

4 Set the oven to broil and return the pork to brown for 10 to 15 minutes, until browned and the skin is bubbly.

5 Slice the roast pork into long strips and cut into thin rectangular pieces. Arrange on a serving platter, garnish with coriander leaves (cilantro) and serve hot or cold with dipping bowls of soy, oyster or hoisin sauce on the side.

Serves 4 to 6   Preparation time: 20 mins + overnight to marinate
Cooking time: 1 hour 15 mins

Pork and Taro Bowl

This is the festive Hakka dish, obligatory for every Hakka celebration. If you have a busy schedule, you can buy roast pork from the nearest Chinese take-away instead of making it. Red preserved bean curd (*nam yee*) has a pungent flavor rather like strong cheese. It comes in cubes packed in jars or bottles and is available in Asian food stores.

Oil for deep-frying
1 taro (about 1 lb/500 g), peeled
  and sliced
1 lb (500 g) roast pork, sliced
1 tablespoon hoisin sauce
1 tablespoon rice wine
1 tablespoon soy sauce
2 tablespoons red preserved
  bean curd (*nam yee*)
1 teaspoon sugar
1 cup (250 ml) water
Sprig of coriander leaves
  (cilantro), to garnish

CRISPY GARLIC
2 tablespoons oil
1 teaspoon sliced garlic

1 Prepare the Crispy Garlic first by heating the oil in a wok over medium heat and stir-frying the garlic for 1 to 2 minutes until fragrant and golden brown. Remove the fried garlic and oil from the pan and set aside.

2 Heat the oil in a wok over medium heat until hot. Deep-fry the taro pieces until golden brown, about 5 minutes. Remove and drain on paper towels.

3 Line a deep bowl or casserole dish with a layer of the pork slices, skin side down, and top with a layer of deep-fried taro pieces. Repeat, alternating the pork and taro layers until both ingredients are used up. Set aside.

4 Combine the Crispy Garlic and oil with all the other ingredients (except the coriander leaves) in a saucepan. Gently heat over medium-low heat until it just boils. Remove from the heat and pour over the pork and taro layers.

5 Set the pork and taro bowl on a steaming rack inside a wok (see page 19) or steamer and steam for about 1 hour. Remove and set aside to cool. Place a serving platter over the bowl or casserole dish and carefully invert the pork and taro onto the serving platter, keeping the pieces neatly layered. Garnish with coriander leaves (cilantro) and serve immediately.

Serves 6 to 8   Preparation time: 25 mins   Cooking time: 1 hour 10 mins

Five Spice Rolls

Five Spice Pork Rolls (*ngo hiang*) are a Fukienese favorite and can be prepared several hours in advance. Keep in the refrigerator until ready to fry. Dried sheets of bean curd skin are traditionally used to wrap them and can be bought from health food stores or Chinese grocers.

1 lb (500 g) lean pork, cut into strips

2 large onions, minced

6 water chestnuts, peeled and diced

4 large sheets dried bean curd skin

2 teaspoons cornstarch, dissolved in 2 tablespoons water

3 cups (750 ml) oil

10 to 12 lettuce leaves, to garnish

Hoisin sauce, for dipping

MARINADE

2 eggs, beaten

2 teaspoons soy sauce

$\frac{1}{2}$ teaspoon five spice powder

$\frac{1}{2}$ teaspoon ground white pepper

1 teaspoon sugar

1 teaspoon salt

SWEET AND SOUR DIP

4 tablespoons Chinese plum sauce

2 tablespoons bottled sweet chili sauce

4 tablespoons sugar

4 tablespoons vinegar

$\frac{1}{4}$ teaspoon salt

1 teaspoon sesame seeds, dry-roasted in a pan for 2 to 3 minutes over low heat

1 Combine the Marinade ingredients in a large bowl and mix well. Place the pork strips and onion in the Marinade and mix until well coated. Allow to marinate for 2 to 3 hours. Add the diced water chestnut to the marinated ingredients, combine well and divide into 16 equal portions.

2 Wipe the dried bean curd skin with a damp cloth to soften them, then cut the sheets into sixteen 6-in (15-cm) squares. Set aside.

3 Prepare the Sweet and Sour Dip by combining all the ingredients (except the sesame seeds) in a serving bowl and mixing well. Scatter the sesame seeds on top and set aside.

4 To make the pork rolls, place a bean curd skin square on a dry surface. Spread a portion of the marinated pork mixture in a straight line along the end of the square nearest you, leaving a 1-in ($2\frac{1}{2}$-cm) edge on either side. Fold the edge of the square nearest you over the filling, then fold in the sides and roll up tightly, pressing firmly as you roll. Before you reach the far edge of the square, lightly dab the inside with the cornstarch solution so it sticks and seals the roll. Continue rolling until the roll forms a tight cylinder. Place the roll on a plate with the seamed side down. Repeat with the remaining ingredients to make a total of 16 pork rolls.

5 Heat the oil in a wok over medium heat until very hot. Carefully lower the pork rolls into the hot oil, a few at a time, and deep-fry for 4 to 5 minutes, turning the rolls until crispy and golden brown on all sides. Remove and drain on paper towels.

6 Slice each roll into disks and arrange them on a serving platter lined with lettuce leaves. Serve hot with dipping bowls of Sweet and Sour Dip, and hoisin sauce on the side.

Makes 16 rolls   Preparation time: 1 hour 15 mins + 3 hours to marinate
Cooking time: 15 mins

Braised Pork Leg

Emblematic of wealth, luck and success, Fatt Choy Chow Sau, the Cantonese name for this recipe, which means "Prosperity at Hand," is just the right dish to put on the festive table. Everything lies in the ingredients. *Fatt choy* (black sea moss) rhymes with "prosperity." Mushrooms are round, symbolic of coins and money. All of these are placed within the "hand," represented by the foreleg of pork. The Cantonese traditionally serve this dish to wish themselves good luck and good fortune on the second day of the Chinese New Year when they hold a noon feast to "open" the year.

1 pork foreleg (3 $^1/_2$ lbs/1 $^1/_2$ kg)

1 tablespoon oil

2 cloves garlic, minced

12 dried black Chinese mushrooms, soaked until soft, stems discarded

1 cup (15 g) dried black sea moss (*fatt choy*), soaked until soft, then rinsed well and squeezed dry

6 dried red dates (*hongzao*) or $^1/_2$ teaspoon sugar

3 cups (750 ml) water

$^1/_2$ teaspoon salt

Sprigs of coriander leaves (cilantro), to garnish

MARINADE

3 tablespoons soy sauce

1 tablespoon black soy sauce

1 tablespoon oyster sauce

1 Sear the pork in an ungreased wok over medium heat for 3 to 4 minutes, turning over once or twice. Remove from the wok and set aside to cool. Combine the Marinade ingredients in a small bowl and mix well. Pour the Marinade over the pork and rub it in with your fingers until the pork is evenly coated. Allow to marinate for at least 30 minutes.

2 Heat the oil in the wok over high heat. Stir-fry the garlic until fragrant and golden brown, 30 seconds. Add the pork and Marinade, mushrooms, black sea moss, red dates or sugar and enough water to cover the pork. Bring the ingredients to a boil, then reduce the heat to medium-low, cover and simmer 1 to 1 $^1/_2$ hours until the pork is tender and the gravy has reduced to half. Season with the salt and remove from the heat.

3 Transfer the pork and other ingredients to a serving platter, and pour the gravy over it. Garnish with coriander leaves (cilantro) and serve hot. If preferred, the gravy may be thickened with 1 teaspoon of cornstarch dissolved in 1 tablespoon of water and simmered for about 1 minute before adding it to the dish.

Serves 6 to 8   Preparation time: 20 mins + 30 mins to marinate
Cooking time: 1 $^1/_2$ hours

Stir-fried Beef with Snow Peas

Cooked this way, beef is both tender and tasty. The addition of snow peas goes very well with the beef. Other vegetables may be added including: bell peppers, spring onions, asparagus, bean sprouts, leeks, tomatoes, kailan, cabbage, mushrooms, bamboo shoots, onions or celery. Combinations of these also work well.

1 cup (100 g) snow peas, tops and tails removed

2 tablespoons oil

1 clove garlic, minced

8 slices fresh young ginger

1 lb (500 g) beef steak, sliced into long thin strips

$\frac{1}{2}$ cup (125 ml) water

1 teaspoon cornstarch dissolved in 1 tablespoon water

MARINADE

2 tablespoons soy sauce

1 tablespoon oyster sauce

$\frac{1}{2}$ teaspoon sugar

$\frac{1}{4}$ teaspoon salt

1 Bring 2 cups (500 ml) of water and $\frac{1}{4}$ teaspoon of salt to a boil over high heat in a small saucepan. Blanch the snow peas for about 30 seconds. Remove from the heat, drain and set aside.
2 Combine the Marinade ingredients in a large bowl and mix well. Add the beef strips and mix until well coated. Marinate for 30 minutes.
3 Heat the oil in a wok over medium heat until very hot. Stir-fry the garlic until fragrant and golden brown, 1 to 2 minutes. Add the ginger and stir-fry for 1 more minute. Add the beef and the Marinade, and stir-fry for 3 to 4 minutes or until the meat changes color. Gather the beef mixture to the sides of the wok and add the water to the center. Bring the water to a boil, pour in the cornstarch solution and combine well. Stir in the beef mixture from the sides and add the snow peas. Stir-fry for 1 minute until the sauce thickens, and remove the dish from the heat.
4 Transfer the dish to a serving platter and serve hot with steamed rice.

Serves 4 to 6   Preparation time: 20 mins + 30 mins to marinate
Cooking time: 10 mins

Pot Roast Beef

This roasting style is very popular in the northern provinces and is often termed "red cooked" — a direct translation of the Cantonese word *hung siew* used to describe the cooking method. The meat may be served hot or cold, and the sauce is normally served separately. Leftover sauce can be saved and used to flavor stocks, stews, soups or meat dishes.

1 tablespoon sugar

3 lbs (1 1/2 kg) stewing beef

2 cloves garlic, bruised

2 in (5 cm) fresh ginger, peeled and thinly sliced

1 star anise pod

1 teaspoon peppercorns

1 cup (250 ml) soy sauce

2 tablespoons black soy sauce

3 tablespoons rice wine

1 teaspoon sesame oil

2 to 3 cups (500 to 750 ml) water

Sprigs of coriander leaves (cilantro), to garnish

1 Caramelize the sugar by heating it in a pot over low heat until it turns golden brown. Add the beef and all the other ingredients (except the coriander leaves) and enough water to cover the beef, and bring to a boil over high heat. Reduce the heat to low and simmer, covered, for 3 to 3 1/2 hours or until the beef is tender. Remove the beef from the saucepan and reserve the sauce. Thinly slice the beef and arrange on a serving platter.

2 Reheat the reserved sauce over medium heat and simmer until it has reduced to about 1 cup (250 ml). Remove from the heat and pour the hot sauce over the beef slices. Garnish with coriander leaves (cilantro) and serve hot with steamed rice.

3 Alternatively, leave the beef and the sauce to cool for 1 1/2 to 2 hours in the saucepan, turning the beef over once. Remove the beef from the pan and thinly slice. Arrange the beef slices on a serving platter, garnish with coriander leaves (cilantro) and serve cold with or without the sauce.

Serves 6 to 8   Preparation time: 10 mins   Cooking time: 3 1/2 hours

Spicy Sichuanese Lamb

Sichuanese recipes literally contain a lot of "ammunition." Dried chilies are liberally used although the quantity can be varied to taste. The chilies are normally not eaten as they are too fiery — they are used only to flavor the sauce — and you should warn your guests to set them aside.

1 lb (500 g) lamb steaks

$^1/_2$ teaspoon salt

2 tablespoons oil

5 dried chilies, broken into 2 to 3 parts and deseeded, soaked until soft, then drained

1 spring onion, sliced diagonally, to garnish

MARINADE

1 clove garlic, crushed

2 tablespoons soy sauce

1 tablespoon oyster sauce

1 tablespoon ginger juice, (from 3 tablespoons grated fresh ginger)

1 tablespoon rice wine

$^1/_2$ teaspoon freshly ground black pepper

$^1/_2$ teaspoon sugar

1 Trim the fat from the lamb and discard. Slice the meat into fairly thin strips. Place in a large bowl and rub the lamb with salt, then set aside.

2 Combine the Marinade ingredients in a mixing bowl and mix well. Place the lamb in the Marinade and mix until well coated. Allow to marinate for at least 1 hour.

3 Heat the oil in a wok over medium heat until smoky hot. Add the chilies and stir-fry until fragrant, about 1 minute. Add the lamb and the Marinade, and stir-fry for 4 to 5 minutes. Increase the heat to high and continue to stir-fry for another 5 to 10 minutes, constantly stirring and turning the ingredients to prevent them from burning, until the sauce is completely absorbed and the meat is dry. Remove from the wok and transfer to a serving platter.

4 Garnish with the spring onion and serve hot with steamed rice.

Serves 4 to 6   Preparation time: 20 mins + 1 hour to marinate
Cooking time: 15 mins

Lamb in Aspic

This is a lovely party dish that can be prepared well in advance and is sure to impress. Use an interesting mold to shape the aspic. Pork skin can be used instead of gelatin to set this dish. Boil a large strip together with the meat. If you use this method, remember not to leave the aspic standing at room temperature for too long or it will start to melt.

7 cups (1³/₄ liters) water

1 lb (500 g) lamb meat, preferably from the leg

1 daikon radish, cubed to yield 2 cups

4 spring onions, trimmed

6 slices fresh ginger

2 cloves garlic

1 star anise

1 small cinnamon stick

1 tablespoon rice wine

4 tablespoons soy sauce

1 teaspoon sugar

1 teaspoon salt

1 baking pan or glass mold

4 teaspoons unflavored gelatin powder

Sweet pickled ginger (see page 38), to serve

DIPPING SAUCE

4 tablespoons sweet bean sauce or hoisin sauce

1 tablespoon bottled chili sauce

1 teaspoon soy sauce

¹/₄ teaspoon sesame oil

¹/₂ teaspoon sesame seeds

1 Bring the water to a boil over high heat in a large pot. Add the lamb and continue to boil for 2 to 3 minutes, skimming off the foam and fat that float to the surface. Add all the other ingredients, except the gelatin and pickled ginger, and return to a boil. Reduce the heat to low and simmer for about 1¹/₂ hours until the meat is tender. Remove the meat from the pot and continue to boil the stock for 20 to 30 minutes, until it reduces to about 1¹/₂ cups (375 ml). Turn off the heat, strain the stock and set aside.

2 Cube the cooked meat and arrange the cubes in a baking pan or mold.

3 In a small saucepan, soak the gelatin in ¹/₄ cup (60 ml) of water for 2 to 3 minutes to soften. Heat the mixture over low heat, stirring occasionally, until the gelatin is dissolved, about 3 minutes. Return the clear stock to a boil over medium heat, then simmer for 2 minutes and stir in the dissolved gelatin. Remove from the heat and pour the thickened stock over the lamb cubes. Set aside to cool, then chill in the refrigerator until set, 4 to 5 hours.

4 While chilling the dish, prepare the Dipping Sauce by combining all the ingredients (except the sesame seeds) in a serving bowl and mixing until smooth. Dry-roast the sesame seeds in an ungreased pan for 2 to 3 minutes over low heat until golden brown, then scatter over the Dipping Sauce.

5 To remove the dish from the mold, run a knife along the edge of the mold to loosen sides. Place a platter over the mold and invert it, shaking gently, to unmold. Serve immediately with sweet pickled ginger and a serving bowl of Dipping Sauce on the side.

Serves 6 to 8   Preparation time: 20 mins + 4 hours chilling
Cooking time: 1 hour 45 mins

Seafood Recipes

Today, seafood, fresh or dried, forms an important part of the Chinese diet. In addition to eating fresh fish, mollusks and crustaceans, the Chinese long ago learned to dry their catch for easier storage and transportation to inland areas. Dried seafood — ranging from the humble salt fish to the highly prized abalone — is not necessarily inferior. It simply develops a different flavor.

Exotic items have always attracted attention. If they also embody an auspicious element, they become even more highly prized as a celebration food. *Haixian* (fresh seafood) and *haiwei* (dried seafood) which fit into this category include oysters (*ho see* in Cantonese, which rhymes with "good events"), black sea moss (*fatt choy* in Cantonese, which rhymes with "booming prosperity") and abalone (*pau yee* in Cantonese, which rhymes with "purse of plenty"), all of which ring with joyful reminders of things the Chinese yearn for — wealth, luck and good fortune.

The top choice for any feast or banquet, however, is still a whole fresh fish — a symbol of plenty — the word *yu* (fish) being synonymous with surplus, excess or bounty. Importantly, the fish must always be cooked and served whole. The Chinese have an abhorrence of the incomplete, more so at celebrations. In traditional families, the dish is placed on the table so that the head points towards the head of the household, the patriarch, who has the honor of selecting the choicest morsels. In the Chinese book of gastronomy, these are the eyes, lips and cheeks. If the patriarch declines, he will delegate the honor to the next most important person at the table, or he may single out a favorite. Another task of the patriarch is to detach the bone from the fish when the top half is eaten; he does this with a deft turn of the chopsticks. Turning the fish over is believed to bring bad luck, a superstition originating among fishing families in southern China who believed their boats would capsize if the fish were treated in this way.

For all their fondness for fish, the Chinese also take pride and satisfaction in a ritual known as *fangsheng* (literally "giving life"), liberating a fish. Any species can be set free but carp, thought to be the favorite of the gods, are the most appropriate. The ritual is usually observed on the second day of the Chinese New Year when a fish is offered to the gods at home or at the temple. After prayers, it is taken in a jar to the river, lake or temple pond and ceremoniously released. To many Chinese, the act of *fangsheng* is a noble and praiseworthy deed, one that heaven will surely note and reward.

Fresh River Carp with Sweet Pickles

Widely used in worship both as ambrosial offerings and cherished icons, river carp are prized
for their endurance and perseverance: they swim upstream against currents and rapids.
In Chinese folklore, the carp that was able to swim all the way up the Yellow River (in China)
and enter the Dragon Gate (a gorge in Shaanxi province) transformed into a resplendent dragon.
The moral of the story: to reap rewards, one must persevere. If carp is not available,
then trout, sea bass or perch may also be used.

1 fresh carp (1 lb/500 g)

$1/2$ teaspoon salt

4 thin slices fresh ginger

2 spring onions, trimmed

$1 1/2$ tablespoons oil

2 cloves garlic, smashed with
the back of a cleaver

1 cup (100 g) sweet Chinese
pickles (see note)

1 finger-length red chili, deseeded
and sliced

1 teaspoon rice wine

$1/2$ cup (125 ml) stock, from the
boiled fish

1 tablespoon vinegar

1 tablespoon sugar

$1/4$ teaspoon salt

1 teaspoon cornstarch, dissolved
in 1 tablespoon water

Dash of sesame oil

Sprigs of coriander leaves
(cilantro), to garnish

Serves 2 to 4
Preparation time: 30 mins
Cooking time: 15 mins

1 Scale, gut and clean the fish, then pat it dry with paper towels.
Rub the salt into the fish and set aside for 15 minutes.
2 In a pot large enough to fit the fish, bring 6 cups ($1 1/2$ liters) of
water to a boil. Add the ginger and spring onions and return to a boil
over high heat, covered. Add the fish, cover the pot tightly and bring
to a boil again. Continue to boil the fish for 2 to 3 minutes, then turn
off the heat and leave the fish in the pot to steep for about 15 minutes.
Remove the fish from the pot, drain and place on a large platter.
Strain the fish stock and reserve $1/2$ cup (125 ml) for the sauce.
3 Heat the oil in a wok over medium heat and stir-fry the garlic until
fragrant, 1 to 2 minutes. Discard the garlic. Add the pickles and
chili, and stir-fry until fragrant, 1 to 2 minutes, seasoning with the
rice wine. Add the fish stock, vinegar, sugar and salt, mix well and
bring the sauce to a boil. Add the cornstarch solution and stir until
the sauce is slightly thickened, about 1 minute, then turn off the
heat. Stir in the sesame oil while the sauce is still simmering. Pour
the hot sauce over the fish, garnish with coriander leaves (cilantro)
and serve immediately.

NOTE: Sweet Chinese pickles such as ginger, leeks, mustard cabbage or papaya
are normally sold in bottles or vacuum-packed in Chinese supermarkets or grocery
stores. You can use a mix or just one type for this dish. If unavailable, sweet
cucumber pickles can be used, or you can make your own by heating $1/2$ cup (125 ml)
vinegar, $1/2$ cup (100 g) sugar and a pinch of salt in a saucepan over low heat for
3 to 5 minutes, stirring until the sugar is dissolved. Bring the mixture to a boil,
then remove from the heat and pour it over 1 cup of thinly sliced vegetable (ginger,
carrot, papaya, cucumber or other non-leafy vegetables). Set aside to cool, then
store in a jar for 2 to 3 days before serving.

Cantonese Steamed Whole Fish

This classic Cantonese-style fish is easy to prepare. Timing is the key. It is also important to use the freshest possible whole fish. Grouper (*shiban*) and pomfret (*changyu*) are the most popular choices. If these are not available, any other firm, white fish can be used.

1 fresh fish (1 lb/500 g)

1/2 teaspoon salt

3 tablespoons oil

2 cloves garlic, minced

1 in (2 1/2 cm) fresh ginger, peeled and cut into fine shreds

1 spring onion, cut into lengths

2 tablespoons soy sauce

1/4 teaspoon sugar

1 finger-length red chili, deseeded and finely sliced, to garnish

1 Scale, gut and clean the fish, then make several shallow diagonal cuts on each side and pat the fish dry with paper towels. Rub the salt into the fish and set aside for 15 minutes.

2 Heat the oil in a wok over medium heat. Stir-fry the garlic until fragrant and golden brown, 1 to 2 minutes. Remove from the heat.

3 Place 1/2 of the ginger shreds and 1/2 of the spring onion on a heat-proof dish, followed by the fish. Combine the fried garlic and oil, soy sauce and sugar in a small bowl and mix well, then pour the mixture over the fish and scatter the remaining ginger shreds on top of the fish. Steam the fish in a covered wok (see page 19) or steamer over high heat for about 15 minutes until the fish is cooked. Remove from the heat.

4 Garnish the steamed fish with sliced chili and remaining spring onion. Serve hot with steamed rice.

Serves 2 to 4   Preparation time: 15 mins   Cooking time: 20 mins

Sweet and Sour Fish

"Sweet and sour" is a popular taste that also appeals to non-Chinese. Green pepper and yellow pineapple look attractive in the tomato-based sauce. Other vegetables such as celery, carrots, green peas and red chilies may also be added.

1 fresh snapper, sea bass or yellow fish (about 1 ½ lbs/700 g)

½ teaspoon salt

1 egg, beaten

4 tablespoons cornstarch

Oil for deep-frying

1 medium onion, sliced

1 green pepper, deseeded and diced to yield about 1 cup

1 cup (5 oz/150 g) fresh or canned pineapple, cubed

Sprigs of coriander leaves (cilantro), to garnish

SWEET AND SOUR SAUCE

3 tablespoons tomato ketchup

1 teaspoon soy sauce

4 teaspoons vinegar

4 teaspoons sugar

5 tablespoons water

½ teaspoon sesame oil

1 Scale, gut and clean the fish, then make several shallow diagonal cuts on each side and pat the fish dry with paper towels. Rub the salt into the fish and set aside for 15 minutes. Using a brush, coat the fish with the beaten egg, then dust it with the cornstarch.

2 Heat the oil in a wok over medium heat until very hot. Gently lower the fish into the hot oil and deep-fry until crispy and golden brown on both sides, 5 to 10 minutes. Remove from the heat and drain on paper towels. Transfer the deep-fried fish to a serving platter.

3 Combine the Sweet and Sour Sauce ingredients in a small bowl and mix well. Set aside.

4 Heat 1 tablespoon of oil in a wok over medium heat until very hot and stir-fry the onion and pepper for about 1 minute. Add the Sweet and Sour Sauce and bring the mixture to a quick boil. Stir-in the pineapple, remove from the heat and spread the mixture over the deep-fried fish. Garnish with coriander leaves (cilantro) and serve hot with steamed rice.

Serves 4   Preparation time: 20 mins   Cooking time: 15 mins

Abalone in Minute Sauce

Abalone is a prized shellfish that suggests, when pronounced in Cantonese, a "purse of plenty." For luck, people fill the "purse" with a bit of "jade," such as parboiled asparagus spears, stems of kailan (Chinese kale) or snow peas. Canned cooked abalone is normally used in Asia as fresh abalone is rarely available. Canned Pacific clams have a similar flavor and are much cheaper. Both are available in Chinese grocery stores.

1 can abalone or Pacific clams

1 cup (100 g) whole snow peas or baby asparagus, trimmed

1 tablespoon oil

$\frac{1}{2}$ cup (125 ml) brine (from the canned abalone or clams)

1 teaspoon rice wine (Shao Xing or Hua Tiew)

$\frac{1}{2}$ teaspoon black soy sauce

$\frac{1}{2}$ teaspoon sugar

$\frac{1}{2}$ teaspoon salt

$\frac{1}{2}$ cup (125 ml) water

1 teaspoon cornstarch, dissolved in 1 tablespoon water

Dash of sesame oil

1 Drain the abalone and reserve $\frac{1}{2}$ cup (125 ml) of the brine for the sauce. Slice each abalone into thick slices. If using Pacific clams, keep them whole.

2 In a saucepan, bring 2 cups (500 ml) of water to a boil over high heat. Blanch the snow peas for 30 seconds or baby asparagus spears for 1 to 2 minutes until tender. Remove from the heat and drain. Set aside.

3 Heat the oil in a wok over medium heat and bring the brine, rice wine, soy sauce, sugar, salt and water to a boil, adjusting the taste with more seasonings as desired. Add the cornstarch solution to the simmering sauce and stir until the sauce thickens slightly, about 1 minute. Add the abalone slices or Pacific clams, mix well and remove from the heat.

4 Place the dish on a serving platter and add a dash of sesame oil. Scatter the snow peas or asparagus spears on top or arrange them around the platter with the abalone or Pacific clams in the center. Serve immediately.

Serves 4   Preparation time: 20 mins   Cooking time: 5 mins

Braised Oysters with Black Sea Moss

The Chinese way of starting the year on the right note is to serve a dish containing auspicious elements. This oyster and sea moss recipe wins hands down; its ingredients reverberating with the sounds of good events and booming prosperity (see page 37).

5 oz (150 g) dried oysters

1 oz (25 g) dried black sea moss

2 tablespoons oil

5 slices fresh ginger

1 spring onion, trimmed

1 tablespoon rice wine or sake

1 tablespoon oyster sauce

2 tablespoons soy sauce

$^1/_2$ teaspoon sugar

1 $^1/_2$ cups (375 ml) dried oyster
   soaking liquid

10 lettuce leaves, blanched for
   10 seconds

$^1/_2$ teaspoon salt

$^1/_4$ teaspoon ground white pepper

$^1/_2$ teaspoon sesame oil

1 teaspoon cornstarch, dissolved
   in 1 tablespoon water

1 Soak the oysters in water for 1 to 2 hours, then drain, reserving 1 $^1/_2$ cups (375 ml) of the soaking water. Set aside.

2 Soak the black sea moss in water for several minutes to soften, then rinse in several changes of water and squeeze dry. Bring a saucepan of water to a boil. Add the black sea moss, 1 teaspoon of the oil and 2 slices of the ginger, and boil for 20 to 30 minutes. Remove from the heat and drain.

3 Heat the remaining oil in a wok over medium heat until very hot. Stir-fry the remaining ginger and spring onion for about 1 minute. Add the oysters and stir-fry for 1 more minute. Season with the rice wine, oyster sauce, soy sauce, sugar and liquid from the soaked oysters. Bring the mixture to a boil, simmer for about 20 minutes and remove from the heat. Discard the ginger and spring onion, drain the oysters and reserve the sauce.

4 Line a wide-rimmed heatproof dish with the cooked oysters in a single layer and fill the center with the sea moss. Pour the reserved sauce over the oysters and cover the bowl with aluminum foil. Steam the dish in a covered wok (see page 19) or steamer for 1 to 1 $^1/_2$ hours. Remove from the heat and drain all the sauce into a small bowl. Place a serving platter over the dish of oysters and sea moss, and carefully invert them onto the serving platter. Arrange the blanched lettuce leaves around the dish.

5 Bring the reserved sauce to a boil over high heat in a saucepan. Add the salt, pepper, sesame oil and cornstarch solution, and mix until the sauce thickens. Remove from the heat, pour the sauce over the dish and serve immediately.

Serves 6 to 8   Preparation time: 30 mins   Cooking time: 2 hours

"Good Luck" Spring Rolls

These delicious rolls are great for parties as most of the preparation can be done in advance. Chill the seafood for 3 to 4 hours in the refrigerator before grinding, or it will be semi-cooked by the heat released during the grinding process.

1 lb (500 g) fresh fish fillets or fresh shrimp

2 tablespoons dried black sea moss

1/2 teaspoon salt

1 teaspoon cornstarch

10 sheets dried bean curd skin, each 4-in (10-cm) square, wiped with a damp cloth to soften

5 salted egg yolks, halved

1 egg, beaten

4 tablespoons fine breadcrumbs

1 teaspoon cornstarch, dissolved in 1 tablespoon water, for sealing

Oil for deep-frying

5 lettuce leaves, to garnish

1 If using shrimp, peel and devein, then rinse thoroughly. Slice the fish or shrimp into pieces and grind to a smooth paste in a food processor. If preferred, you may mince the seafood using a cleaver.

2 Soak the black sea moss in water for several minutes to soften, then rinse well and squeeze dry. In a large bowl, combine the ground or minced seafood with the sea moss, salt and cornstarch, stirring in one direction until the mixture pulls away from the sides of the bowl. Wet your hands, gather and shape the mixture into a ball and slap it repeatedly against the inside of the bowl until the mixture is smooth and "springy" to the touch. Divide the mixture into 10 equal portions.

3 To make the rolls, place a bean curd skin sheet on a dry surface. Spread 1 portion of the seafood mixture in a straight line along the end of the square nearest you, leaving 1 in (2 1/2 cm) on either side, and place an egg yolk halve on top. Fold the end of the sheet over the filling, then fold in the two sides and roll up tightly, pressing firmly as you roll. Before you reach the end of the square, lightly dab the inside edge with a bit of the cornstarch solution. Continue rolling and seal the roll into a tight cylinder, about 2 in (5 cm) in length. Place the roll on a heatproof dish with the seamed side down. Repeat with the remaining ingredients to make a total of 10 rolls.

4 Steam the rolls in a covered wok (see page 19) or steamer over high heat for 15 to 20 minutes. Remove from the heat and set aside to cool.

5 Heat the oil in a wok over medium heat until hot. Working with a few at a time, dip the rolls in the beaten egg and roll in a plate of breadcrumbs until well coated. Carefully lower the coated rolls into the hot oil and deep-fry for 2 to 3 minutes, turning the rolls until crispy and golden brown on all sides. Remove and drain on paper towels.

6 Halve each roll and arrange on a serving platter lined with a bed of lettuce leaves. Serve hot or cold.

Makes 10 rolls   **Preparation time: 1 hour**   **Cooking time: 30 mins**

Vegetable Recipes

It is astonishing how the names of foods in Chinese take on the sounds and symbolism of things the Chinese have traditionally associated with good life. Even the generic name for any humble vegetable – *choy* – has an auspicious ring to it: the sound of wealth and fortune. As if sounds were not enough, there is color to complete the imagery. *Choy* (Cantonese for vegetable) or *cai* (Mandarin for vegetable) comes in the colors of all things valuable – jade, gold and ivory – to complete the celebratory theme.

Sounds and symbols aside, vegetables pack fiber and minerals in their leaves, stalks, pods and bulbs. Many vegetables have long been used in folk cures, an integral part of Chinese culture and one which commands a large following today despite advances in modern medical science. To this day, people eat okra to speed up recovery from an attack of jaundice. Celery is taken to reduce blood pressure, and boiled daikon to relieve headaches. Nursing mothers are given plenty of ginger, believed to restore the womb and strengthen it for further reproduction. Ginger is also considered good for digestion and, best of all, for expelling "wind" – the culprit, according to folk diagnoses, for a wide range of ailments. Garlic, chives, watercress, lotus root, water chestnuts – all these help keep the body healthy by flushing toxins from the bloodstream, dissolving blood clots or giving organs a good "cleansing." Exactly how this is done, grandmother does not say. Research, however, has shown that vegetables contain detoxifiers, antioxidants, diuretics and anticarcinogens, suggesting that grandmother's home-cures have a scientific basis after all.

With so much going for them, it is unwise to omit vegetables from offerings to the gods. Household gods are particularly fond of lettuce (which is said to have narcotic qualities), celery and spring onions. Happily, the word for lettuce (*shengcai*) suggests life, growth and wealth. Spring onions (*cong*) and celery (*qincai*) signify intelligence and wisdom respectively, the hollowness of their stalks interpreted as unimpaired vision. Fresh, whole bunches of the three vegetables, trimmed with strips of red paper for luck, are offered to the gods together with chicken, roast pork and any number of other delicacies. Afterwards, the vegetables are used as garnishes or eaten with leftovers for the traditional post-festival dish, *chop suey*.

Mixed Vegetables with Lobster

All the colors associated with things of great value and splendor — jade, gold and ivory —
are contained in this dish, plus the luxury of lobster. If your budget does not extend to lobster,
you may substitute shrimp or sliced squid for lobster.

1 fresh lobster (about 2 lbs/900 g)

2 tablespoons oil

2 cloves garlic, minced

1 tablespoon thinly sliced fresh
   ginger

10 asparagus spears, sliced diagonally into bite-sized lengths

1 1/2 cups (150 g) cauliflower florets

1 carrot, sliced to yield 1 1/2 cups

1 finger-length red chili, deseeded
   and sliced diagonally into strips

2 tablespoons soy sauce

1 teaspoon oyster sauce

1/2 teaspoon sugar

3 tablespoons water

1/4 teaspoon ground white pepper

1 Detach the head of the lobster from the body. Turn the body on its
back and using a sharp knife or kitchen scissors, split the shell
lengthwise down the center, starting from the head. Pull away the
shell to obtain the meat. Crack the large claws with a nutcracker and
carefully remove the meat. Discard the shell. Cut the lobster meat
into large chunks.

2 Heat the oil in a wok over high heat until smoky hot. Stir-fry the
garlic and ginger for 30 seconds until fragrant and golden brown. Add
the lobster meat and stir-fry for 1 to 2 minutes until pink and just
cooked. Add all the vegetables and continue to stir-fry for 2 minutes,
then season with the soy sauce, oyster sauce and sugar. Add the water,
mix well and simmer covered for about 2 minutes until the vegetables
are tender. Finally add the pepper and remove from the heat.
Transfer to a serving platter and serve hot with steamed rice.

Serves 4 to 6   Preparation time: 30 mins   Cooking time: 10 mins

Kailan with Crabmeat Sauce

Firm, crunchy greens are best for this recipe. Kailan (Chinese kale) is the most popular choice but asparagus, broccoli and mustard cabbage can be used instead. A very good stock prepared from meat bones and bacon is recommended (see page 57).

1 lb (500 g) kailan (Chinese kale)
4 cups (1 liter) water
$^1/_4$ teaspoon salt

CRABMEAT SAUCE
1 cup (250 ml) Chicken and Pork
    Stock (see page 57) or normal
    chicken stock
$^1/_4$ teaspoon salt
1 cup (150 g) cooked crabmeat
1 egg, beaten
1 teaspoon cornstarch, dissolved in
    1 tablespoon water
Pinch of ground white pepper
Dash of sesame oil

1 Prepare the kailan by trimming and discarding the old leaves, keeping only the young tender shoots. Trim the young shoots from the main stems. Peel the bottom parts of the main stems, then slice the stems diagonally. Set aside.

2 In a saucepan, bring the water and salt to a boil over medium heat. Boil the kailan stems for about 1 minute, followed by the young shoots for about 10 seconds. Turn off the heat and leave the vegetable in the pot to steep for 2 to 3 minutes. Drain and arrange the boiled kailan on a serving platter.

3 To make the Crabmeat Sauce, bring the stock to a boil over medium heat in a small saucepan. Season with the salt, add the crabmeat and egg, and mix well. Add the cornstarch solution and stir until the sauce has thickened, about 1 minute. Finally add the pepper and sesame oil, mix well and remove from the heat. Pour the hot sauce over the boiled kailan and serve immediately with steamed rice.

Serves 4   Preparation time: 15 mins   Cooking time: 5 mins

Chinese Lettuce Leaf Cups

Soft leaf lettuces are best for this provincial dish from the south. Dab a piece of leaf with chili or hoisin sauce, fill it with a spoonful of the cooked ingredients, bunch it up and pop it into the mouth. Dried cuttlefish or squid is sold whole or in processed strips. The whole fish must be soaked for hours until soft before slicing. Dried shrimp may be used instead of dried cuttlefish or squid.

$1/3$ cup (about 25 g) sliced dried cuttlefish or squid, or $1/3$ cup (40 g) dried shrimp

4 oz (120 g) pork belly

2 tablespoons oil

1 shallot, very finely sliced

1 medium *bangkuang* (jicama), peeled and cut into thin shreds to yield 3 cups

1 carrot, coarsely grated to yield $1^1/_2$ cups

10 green beans, sliced diagonally into thin shreds

2 tablespoons soy sauce

5 tablespoons water

Pinch of salt

3 tablespoons coarsely ground roasted unsalted peanuts, to garnish (optional)

1 small head lettuce, leaves separated

Bottled sweet chili sauce or hoisin sauce, to serve

1 Soak the dried cuttlefish or squid in warm water until soft, then drain well. Thinly slice the whole fish into short lengths. Set aside. If using dried shrimp, soak them in water for about 15 minutes until soft, then drain well and chop them with a cleaver or grind coarsely in a blender.

2 Skin the pork belly and discard the skin. Mince the pork with a cleaver or grind it in a food processor until fine. Set aside.

3 Heat the oil in a wok over high heat until smoky hot. Stir-fry the shallot until translucent and tender, about 30 seconds. Add the pork and dried seafood, and stir-fry for about 2 minutes. Add the vegetables and stir-fry for 2 more minutes. Season with the soy sauce, water and salt, and mix well. Reduce the heat to medium and simmer for about 15 minutes, or until the vegetables are tender and the sauce has been absorbed. Adjust the seasoning with more soy sauce or water as desired, and remove from the pan.

4 Place the dish on a serving platter and top with ground peanuts (if using). Serve hot or chilled with lettuce leaves and serving bowls of chili or hoisin sauce on the side.

Serves 4 to 6   Preparation time: 40 mins + 2 hours soaking
Cooking time: 25 mins

Tossed Greens in Garlic Flavored Sauce

This is a simple recipe that can be used for almost any kind of vegetable: asparagus, snow peas, mustard cabbage, lettuce, bean sprouts, string beans, broccoli, bok choy, kailan, Brussels sprouts, spinach, and more if you experiment.

4 cups (1 liter) water

¹/₄ teaspoon salt

1 lb (500 g) vegetable of your choice, washed and drained

GARLIC FLAVORED SAUCE

2 tablespoons oil

2 cloves garlic, minced

1¹/₂ tablespoons soy sauce

1 teaspoon oyster sauce

2 tablespoons chicken stock or stock from the blanched vegetables

¹/₂ teaspoon sugar

1 Prepare the Garlic Flavored Sauce first by heating the oil in a wok over high heat until smoky hot. Stir-fry the garlic for 30 seconds until fragrant and golden brown. Remove the garlic and oil from the wok and set aside to cool, then combine with all the other ingredients and mix well. (If using the stock from the blanched vegetables, add the required amount later, before tossing the blanched vegetables.)

2 In a saucepan, bring the water and salt to a boil over medium heat, and briefly blanch the vegetables (about 30 seconds for bean sprouts, 1 minute for snow peas or spinach, and 2 to 3 minutes for asparagus, mustard cabbage or broccoli). Remove the blanched vegetables from the heat, drain and place on a serving platter.

3 Pour the Garlic Flavored Sauce over the blanched vegetables and using a pair of chopsticks, gently toss to mix well. Serve immediately.

Serves 4   Preparation time: 10 mins   Cooking time: 5 mins

Braised Assorted Vegetables

You can play with different combinations in this recipe, an adaptation on the traditional Buddhist vegetarian dish, *lohanzai*. In addition to the ingredients below, you can add a variety of mushrooms and cabbages. Black sea moss, dried bean curd sticks, lotus root, carrots, bamboo shoots and gingko nuts are popular additions. You can also leave out the dried oysters for a purely vegetarian version of this dish.

$^1/_2$ cup (50 g) dried oysters

6 dried black Chinese mushrooms

3 tablespoons dried cloud
  ear fungus

$^1/_2$ cup (20 g) dried lily buds

2 small bundles (25 g each) dried
  glass noodles

3 tablespoons oil

15 snow peas, tops and tails
  removed

6 water chestnuts, peeled and
  sliced

$1^1/_2$ cups (150 g) Chinese
  cabbage, washed and cut into
  thin shreds

1 tablespoon preserved red bean
  curd (see note)

2 tablespoons soy sauce

1 teaspoon oyster sauce

$^1/_2$ teaspoon sugar

$^1/_2$ teaspoon salt

Serves 4 to 6
Preparation time: 30 mins + 1 hour
  soaking
Cooking time: 20 mins

1 Prepare all of the dried ingredients first. Soak the dried oysters in warm water for about 1 hour, then drain and reserve $^1/_2$ cup (125 ml) of the soaking liquid. Soak the Chinese mushrooms in hot water for about 30 minutes, then drain and reserve $^1/_2$ cup (125 ml) of the soaking liquid. Remove and discard the stems and slice the caps into strips. Soak the cloud ear fungus and lily buds for 15 minutes in warm water, then drain and discard the hard ends. Tear or cut the cloud ear fungus into 2 or 3 pieces each. Soak the glass noodles in water for 10 minutes, then drain. Set all the soaked ingredients on a large plate or cutting board.

2 Heat 1 tablespoon of the oil in a wok over high heat until hot. Briefly stir-fry the snow peas in the hot oil for about 30 seconds, then remove and set aside.

3 Heat the remaining oil in the wok over medium heat. Add the oysters, mushroom strips, cloud ear fungus, lily buds, water chestnuts and cabbage, and stir-fry for 2 to 3 minutes, seasoning with the preserved red bean curd or hoisin sauce, soy sauce, oyster sauce and sugar. Add the reserved oyster and mushroom soaking liquid, mix well and bring the mixture to a boil. Add the glass noodles, cover and simmer for 8 to 10 minutes. Finally season with the salt, stir in the snow peas, cook for 1 minute and remove from the pan. Transfer to a serving platter and serve immediately.

NOTE: Preserved red bean curd is the red variety of preserved bean curd, normally sold in cans or jars in Chinese grocery stores. Unlike the beige variety, these little red cheeselike cubes contain red rice lees that gives a red color. Once opened, it must be refrigerated.

Steamed Vegetable Platter

Attractively arranged vegetables always look interesting and tempting.
Broccoli or kailan can be used instead of bok choy.

10 dried black Chinese mushrooms
10 baby corn ears
10 baby bok choy sprouts,
  blanched for 2 to 3 minutes
$1/_2$ carrot, sliced

SAUCE
2 tablespoons oil
1 clove garlic, minced
1 cup (250 ml) mushroom soaking
  liquid or chicken stock
1 tablespoon soy sauce
$1/_2$ teaspoon sugar
$1/_4$ teaspoon salt
1 teaspoon cornstarch, dissolved in
  1 tablespoon water

1 Rinse the mushrooms well, then soak in hot water until soft, about
30 minutes. Drain and reserve 1 cup (250 ml) of the soaked liquid.
Remove and discard the stems from the mushrooms. Rinse the
mushrooms well, then squeeze dry.

2 Arrange the vegetables in a heatproof dish with the mushrooms in
the center, surrounded by the baby corn and bok choy forming the
outer ring. Fill a wok with 6 cups ($1 1/_2$ liters) of water and bring it to
a boil over high heat. Place a metal rack in the wok and set the dish
of vegetables on top of the rack, making sure that it does not touch
the boiling water. Cover the wok tightly and steam the vegetables for
15 to 20 minutes. Alternatively, steam the vegetables in a steamer if
you own one.

3 While steaming the vegetables, prepare the Sauce by heating the
oil in a wok over high heat and stir-frying the garlic until fragrant and
golden brown, about 30 seconds. Add the stock, soy sauce, sugar and
salt, and bring the mixture to a boil. Add the cornstarch solution and
stir for about 1 minute, or until the Sauce slightly thickens. Remove
from the heat, pour the hot Sauce over the vegetables and serve
immediately.

Serves 4 to 6   Preparation time: 15 mins + 30 mins soaking
Cooking time: 25 mins

Rice, Soups and Noodles

Rice is the staple food of the Chinese. It is the food most intimately linked with life and is thus treated with a respect bordering on reverence. If rice is spilled on the floor, it is not swept away but picked up grain by grain. The household rice store is synonymous with luck and prosperity. Chinese housewives deplore running out of rice as this signifies "out of luck," which interrupts prosperity. For the same reason, the measuring cup is never left empty but some grains are left inside when it is returned to the storage jar, to ensure uninterrupted prosperity. Rice is too precious to waste, so every grain is eaten. Chinese children learn at an early age to leave their rice bowls clean. If they do not, they will, according to their mothers and grandmothers, "get married to pock-marked spouses."

Naturally, the gods and ancestors have to be sustained with rice, and on feast days white rice is offered in small bowls as part of the ambrosial spread. Chopsticks are set in position pointing at the food (chopsticks circumnavigate the table for mortals), along with tiny cups of wine. Gods need a little wine to help them get into the party mood.

In the traditional family feast, rice is also a prerequisite, and is eaten with many dishes cooked in various ways and placed together on the table. Everyone is free to help himself. The family feast is not a formal dinner. There are no fixed rules and food may be taken in any order or in any combinations.

A soup dish is certain to be included in the menu. For gods, this is not obligatory, though a tasty soup will always be welcome. The soup is invariably a clear soup with plenty of flavor: meat or poultry boiled together with vegetables, seeds or dried seafood such as oysters, scallops and sea cucumbers. The soup is not served as a separate course. Rather, it is sipped in spoonfuls in between mouthfuls of the other dishes. It takes the place of water, which is never served at the Chinese table. Only luxurious thick or creamy soups, such as shark's fin, are consumed by themselves and at banquets are always served at the beginning of a meal.

A "sustaining starch" dish is normally served at the end to fill up any remaining empty spaces — usually a fried rice or noodle dish. Noodles are a must when celebrating birthdays. The Chinese eat a great variety of noodles: fresh, dried, processed from wheat, rice or beans. For birthdays, however, wheat noodles (*mian*) are the preferred fare as they signify longevity. To be true to custom, noodles should be eaten as served: that is, the strands should not be broken while eating, no matter how unmanageable as this is unlucky.

Shark's Fin Soup

Preparing dried shark's fins for cooking is a tedious task, involving long hours of cleaning, soaking and boiling. Fortunately, it is now possible to buy frozen, ready-prepared shark's fins from the supermarket. In an effort to protect sharks from extinction due to over-fishing, always purchase ecologically friendly shark's fins harvested from non-endangered species.

If you cannot find them, you may want to try a "mock shark's fin" using vegetarian shark's fins or glass noodles as a substitute. These taste just as good. The secret of a good shark's fin soup lies in the stock. A stock prepared from a combination of chicken, pork and bacon or air-dried ham is recommended. Yunnan ham is the traditional choice but you can also use Parma ham or Canadian bacon.

2 tablespoons oil

7 oz (200 g) prepared shark's fin or $^1/_2$ cup (35 g) dried glass noodles, soaked until soft, then cut into lengths

4 oz (120 g) cooked crabmeat

3 tablespoons water chestnut flour or cornstarch, dissolved in 4 tablespoons water

1 egg, beaten

Dash of sesame oil

Black vinegar, to serve (optional)

CHICKEN AND PORK STOCK

12 cups (3 liters) water

1 lb (500 g) pork ribs

10 oz (300 g) chicken breasts

10 oz (300 g) Yunnan or Parma ham or back bacon

Sprigs of coriander leaves (cilantro)

Salt to taste

1 Prepare the Chicken and Pork Stock first by bringing the water to a boil over high heat in a stockpot. Add all the other ingredients (except the salt) and return to a boil. Continue to boil for about 5 minutes, then reduce the heat to low, cover and simmer for 1 to 1$^1/_2$ hours until the stock reduces to half (6 cups/1$^1/_2$ liters). Season with the salt and remove from the heat. Strain the stock. Reserve the stock and chicken meat in separate containers.

2 Shred the cooked chicken meat (from the stock) along the grain into thin strips. Set aside.

3 Heat the oil in a wok over high heat until smoky hot. Pour in the stock and bring to a boil. Stir in the shark's fin (or glass noodles), reduce the heat to medium and simmer uncovered for about 10 minutes (or 3 minutes if using glass noodles). Add the chicken strips and crabmeat and mix well. Add the water chestnut flour or cornstarch solution and stir until the soup thickens. Slowly pour in the beaten egg while stirring the stock, then add the sesame oil, and remove from the heat.

4 Ladle the Shark's Fin Soup into individual serving bowls. Serve hot with a bowl of black vinegar (if using) on the side.

Serves 4 to 6   Preparation time: 30 mins   Cooking time: 1 hour 45 mins

Winter Melon Soup

Light, clear soups are an excellent accompaniment to the traditional Chinese feast. This double-boiled recipe uses a whole winter melon as a container for the soup. To impress your guests, hand-carve the melon. Even a simple zigzag border along the top of the melon can be interesting.

1 small winter melon, about 4 lbs /2 kg

4 oz (120 g) fresh boneless chicken meat, cubed

3 dried black Chinese mushrooms, soaked in hot water until soft, stems discarded, caps diced

8 dried scallops ($\frac{1}{3}$ cup/40 g), rinsed and drained

8 dried oysters ($\frac{1}{2}$ cup/50 g), rinsed and drained

4 dried red dates, pitted

3 cups (750 ml) boiling water

Toothpicks, for fastening

$\frac{1}{2}$ teaspoon salt

Serves 4
Preparation time: 30 mins
Cooking time: 1 $\frac{1}{2}$ hours

1 Stand the melon on a flat surface. Using a pencil and at eye level, make a few markings around the melon at about a quarter height of the melon from the top. On a cutting board, place the melon on its side and along the markings, cut out the top section of the melon to form the "lid." Scoop out the seeds and pulp from the melon until its wall is about $\frac{3}{4}$ in (2 cm) thick. Discard the seeds and pulp, and hand-carve the melon if desired. Place the melon in a heatproof dish.
2 Combine all the other ingredients (except the salt) in a large bowl, mix well and pour into the melon. Replace the "lid" and secure it with toothpicks. Set the dish with the melon on a rack in a large wok (see page 19) or steamer, and steam over medium heat for 1 to 1 $\frac{1}{2}$ hours. Alternatively, wrap the melon with plastic wrap and microwave it for 40 to 50 minutes at medium. Remove from the heat, season with the salt and serve hot.

NOTE: You can also prepare this delicious soup very quickly by removing the skin and seeds from the melon, cutting the flesh into chunks and double-boiling with all the other ingredients in a double boiler for 1 $\frac{1}{2}$ hours. If you do not own a double boiler, place the melon chunks and all the other ingredients in a deep, heatproof bowl. Stand the dish on a rack in a large covered wok and steam over medium heat for the same period of time.

Fried Rice in a Lotus Leaf

When dinner is a formal, multicourse affair, it is customary to serve the "filler" before the dessert. The all-time favorite is fried rice served in a lotus leaf, a hearty dish that may be eaten as a meal in itself. You can use either a fresh or dried leaf, but dry ones are more readily available from Chinese grocers. Before using, soak the dried leaf in hot water until it is softened.

1 ¹/₂ cups (375 ml) water

5 oz (150 g) boneless chicken meat

3 tablespoons oil

¹/₂ teaspoon sesame oil

1 clove garlic, minced

2 shallots, diced

1 teaspoon grated fresh ginger

¹/₂ cup (60 g) dried shrimp, soaked for 15 minutes, drained and ground in a mortar or blender

5 cups (500 g) cooked white rice

2 dried Chinese sausages (*lap cheong*) or 3 pieces ham, diced

6 dried black Chinese mushrooms, soaked until soft, stems discarded, caps thinly sliced

2 tablespoons soy sauce

1 teaspoon black soy sauce

¹/₂ teaspoon sugar

¹/₂ teaspoon ground white pepper

¹/₂ teaspoon salt

1 large fresh or dried lotus leaf, wiped clean and soaked in hot water to soften

Serves 4 to 6
Preparation time: 30 mins
Cooking time: 1 hour

1 Bring the water to a boil over medium heat in a small saucepan and poach the chicken for about 15 minutes until cooked. Remove the chicken from the pan and set aside to cool. Shred the chicken along the grain into fine strips.

2 Heat both types of oil in a wok over high heat until smoky hot. Stir-fry the garlic, shallot and ginger until fragrant and golden brown, about 30 seconds. Add the dried shrimp and stir-fry for 1 to 2 minutes. Add all the other ingredients (except the lotus leaf) and stir-fry until heated through and well blended, 2 to 3 minutes. Remove the fried rice from the heat and place on a platter.

3 Shake the water off the lotus leaf and spread it on a flat surface with the smooth side up. Place the fried rice in the center of the leaf while it is still hot. Wrap into a neat package by folding the sides of the leaf inwards and over the rice on 4 sides, securing with toothpicks or kitchen string. Place the package in a heatproof dish with the folded side facing down, and steam it on a rack in a covered wok (see page 19) or steamer over high heat for 45 minutes to 1 hour. Remove from the heat and transfer to a serving dish.

4 Cut a round hole out of the top of the package with a pair of kitchen scissors and scoop out the rice to serve.

NOTE: If you cannot find a lotus leaf, use aluminum foil instead.

Yangzhou Fried Rice

Fried rice makes a good one dish meal. It can also be served as a final course at the end of a formal dinner.

4 cups (400 g) cold cooked rice
1 tablespoon oil
2 spring onions, minced
1 tablespoon minced fresh ginger
4 oz (120 g) fresh medium shrimp, peeled and deveined, halved
1 cup (5 oz/150 g) fresh or frozen peas, blanched (3 minutes for fresh or 5 minutes for frozen)
2 eggs, beaten
1 teaspoon Shao Xing rice wine
1 tablespoon soy sauce
$\frac{1}{2}$ teaspoon salt
$\frac{1}{4}$ teaspoon freshly ground black pepper
$1\frac{1}{2}$ tablespoons chicken stock
$\frac{1}{4}$ teaspoon sesame oil
Sprigs of coriander leaves (cilantro), to garnish

1 Place the rice in a large bowl and use a spoon to break up the lumps and separate the grains. Set aside.

2 Heat the oil in a wok over high heat until hot. Stir-fry the spring onion and ginger until fragrant, about 30 seconds. Add the shrimp and blanched peas, and stir-fry until the shrimp turn pink. Reduce the heat to medium, add the eggs and scramble lightly.

3 Before the eggs are completely set, add the cooked rice. Increase the heat to high, toss and turn the rice very quickly with the spatula until the rice is heated through and the grains are well separated, 30 seconds to 1 minute. Season with the wine, soy sauce, salt and pepper and mix until well blended. Add half of the chicken stock and stir-fry for 30 seconds. Pour in the remaining chicken stock and continue stir-frying for another 30 seconds. Finally add the sesame oil to the fried rice, toss well and remove from the heat.

4 Transfer the fried rice to a serving platter, garnish with coriander leaves (cilantro) and serve immediately.

Serves 3 to 4   Preparation time: 20 mins   Cooking time: 5 mins

Rice Threads with Pork and Bean Sprouts

There is no rule against serving noodles together with rice at the same meal. In fact, the Chinese like a lot of carbohydrate "fillers" to make sure nobody goes home hungry (or anything less than stuffed). Except on birthdays, any variety can be cooked. This rice noodle recipe is quick and easy. The pork mixture can be prepared well ahead and the noodles can be tossed just before serving.

10 oz (300 g) ground pork

$1/_2$ teaspoon salt

$1/_2$ teaspoon ground white pepper

10 oz (300 g) dried rice noodles, soaked in water for 15 minutes

6 cups (10 oz/300 g) bean sprouts

4 spring onions, cut into lengths

4 tablespoons oil

10 shallots, thinly sliced to yield about 5 tablespoons

1 finger-length red chili, deseeded and sliced, to garnish

DRESSING

3 tablespoons soy sauce

1 tablespoon black soy sauce

1 tablespoon oyster sauce

$3/_4$ cup (185 ml) chicken stock

3 tablespoons shallot oil (from the fried shallots above)

1 teaspoon sesame oil

1 Brown the pork in a heated wok or skillet over medium heat for about 5 minutes until cooked, and season with the salt and pepper, tossing lightly to combine. If preferred, add a few drops of black soy sauce for a richer color. Remove and set aside.

2 Bring a pot of water to a boil over medium heat. Add the rice noodles and cook for 7 to 8 minutes, or until tender. Remove from the pot, then drain and set aside.

3 Bring a pot of water and $1/_4$ teaspoon of salt to a boil over medium heat. Remove the tops and tails from the bean sprouts and blanch them and the spring onion for 30 seconds. Remove from the pot, drain and set aside.

4 Heat the oil in a wok or skillet over medium heat and stir-fry the shallots for 2 to 3 minutes until golden brown and crispy. Drain the fried shallots and reserve the oil. Set aside.

5 Make the Dressing by combining all the ingredients in a bowl and mixing well. Set aside.

6 Place the noodles, bean sprouts, spring onion and $1/_2$ of the ground pork in a large serving platter. Pour the Dressing over the noodles and toss until all the ingredients are evenly coated. Spread the remaining pork and the fried shallots on top, garnish with red chili strips and serve immediately.

Serves 4 to 6   Preparation time: 30 mins   Cooking time: 20 mins

Braised Longevity Noodles

To secure the virtues of longevity, the Chinese serve noodles on birthdays. Only
wheat noodles — the embodiment of length and strength — satisfy the requirements of this dish,
as rice noodles break too easily. Any variety of fresh or dried wheat noodles may be used:
egg noodles, *yeefumian*, Hokkien *mee* or the special birthday "long life" noodles (*changshoumian*),
which come in a long box. If using dried noodles for this recipe,
cook first as instructed on the package.

8 oz (250 g) fresh shrimp, peeled
and deveined
1 lb (500 g) fresh wheat noodles
or 8 oz (250 g) dried noodles
2 tablespoons oil
1 clove garlic, minced or crushed
7 oz (200 g) lean pork or chicken,
sliced into strips
4 leaves Chinese cabbage, cut
into thin shreds
1 medium carrot, thinly sliced
1 bunch (4 oz/120 g) Chinese
chives, cut into lengths
6 dried black Chinese mushrooms
$1/_2$ cup (125 ml) chicken stock or
mushroom soaking water
2 tablespoons soy sauce
1 tablespoon oyster sauce
$1/_4$ teaspoon salt
1 teaspoon cornstarch, dissolved
in 1 tablespoon water
1 piece (4 oz/120 g) dried fish,
deep-fried, then crushed
(optional)
1 finger-length red chili, deseeded
and sliced

1 Rub a dash of sugar into the peeled shrimp and set aside. Soak the Chinese mushrooms in hot water for 30 minutes until soft, then drain, reserving $1/_2$ cup (125 ml) of the liquid (if using). Remove and discard the stems and slice the caps.
2 Bring a pot of water to a boil over medium heat. Add the wheat noodles and cook for about 2 minutes (5 minutes for the dried noodles), stirring and loosening as they cook with a chopstick or fork. Remove from the heat and immediately plunge the noodles into a basin of cold water to cool, then strain and set aside.
3 Heat the oil in a wok over high heat until smoky hot. Stir-fry the garlic until fragrant and golden brown, about 30 seconds. Add the shrimp and stir-fry until pink and just cooked, 1 to 2 minutes, then add the pork or chicken strips and vegetables, and stir-fry for 2 more minutes. Pour in the stock or soaking liquid and bring the mixture to a boil. Add the noodles, mix well and season with the soy sauce, oyster sauce and salt, then return to a boil. Finally add the cornstarch solution and mix until well blended and the sauce has thickened, about 1 minute. Turn off the heat and transfer the noodles to a serving platter.
4 Top the noodles with crushed deep-fried fish flakes (if using) and sliced chili. Serve immediately.

Serves 4 to 6   Preparation time: 45 mins   Cooking time: 10 mins

Dessert Recipes

The sweet dish we have come to expect at the end of a Chinese feast is cosmopolitan in character, evidence that the Middle Kingdom has been exposed to many outside influences. For a long time, the Chinese were content to end a meal with fresh fruit. Sometimes dried fruits, seeds and nuts prepared in a clear sweet broth are offered in addition, many of which are said to have digestive or restorative properties. Many dessert dishes have evolved through continuous exposure to outside cultures. Today, no one is surprised if a jelly, pudding or ice cream is served in place of the traditional fruits and soups.

Cakes and pastries, too, have found their way to the Chinese table. The Treaty of Nanjing, which forced China to open its ports to the international community in the mid-19th century, initiated a culinary invasion of sorts. Butter cream cakes, tarts and crepes are some of the more cheerful, albeit rarely mentioned, developments of the treaty.

Traditional Chinese cakes are steamed rather than baked and rice flour is widely used. Pastries, too, rarely come out of the oven: steaming and deep-frying are the preferred methods. Sweetmeat, if used, typically consists of ground preparations of seeds, nuts and dates. The use of bright colors in festive confectionary is widespread in keeping with their role as offerings for the gods. Pink and red are commonly used as these convey joy and luck. Some of these traditional cakes are served as dessert dishes in restaurants today, but generally they are regarded as *dianxin* — snack foods associated with teahouses as well as the homely rice cakes and pastries the Chinese eat in between meals or at any time of the day or night.

Household gods appear to follow a similar eating pattern and show a distinct preference for rice cakes. On festival days, a variety of these are left on the altar for celestial guests to snack on while waiting for the party to begin. No ceremony needs to accompany this minor offering. Ceremony is only obligatory for the main offerings: the splendid feast of chicken, pork and other cooked dishes that follow. Nobody makes a fuss over the dessert, and fresh fruit and rice cakes are offered as they have been for generations. Approval is certain. Unlike the Chinese people, their gods have yet to succumb to the Western traditions of puddings and cream cakes.

"Four Treasures" in a Clear Sweet Soup

Traditionally, dried longans are used in this recipe to provide a tonic brew, believed to fortify the body and improve circulation. As a dessert, however, canned longans are preferred as they taste better. Whipped cream may be added on top just before serving.

½ cup (70 g) dried gingko nuts
½ cup (60 g) dried lotus seeds
½ cup (50 g) dried magnolia petals (see note)
6 cups (1½ liters) water
¾ cup (150 g) sugar
1 can longans or lychees, drained

Serves 4
Preparation time: 30 mins + 30 mins soaking
Cooking time: 40 mins

1 Shell the gingko nuts by cracking each one with a pestle or nut-cracker and removing the shell. Peel off the papery skins using a paring knife. Halve each nut and discard the endosperm (central core), which is bitter. Do the same to the lotus seeds.

2 Soak the gingko nuts, lotus seeds and magnolia petals in separate bowls in cold water for about 30 minutes, then drain.

3 In a pot, bring the gingko nuts, lotus seeds, magnolia petals and water to a boil over high heat. Lower the heat to medium, simmer uncovered for about 20 minutes until the ingredients are tender. Add the sugar and stir gently until the sugar is dissolved. Continue to simmer for another 10 to 15 minutes, then remove from the heat and set aside to cool. Add the longans, mix well and chill in the refrigerator.

4 Spoon the chilled dessert into individual serving bowls and serve.

NOTE: Magnolia petals are petals of the Chinese magnolia flowers. Used mostly in tonics or soups, they are available dried in Chinese herbalist shops.

Sago Pearls with Honeydew Melon

A light, refreshing dessert like this one is the perfect finish to a Chinese meal. Sago beads or tapioca pearls are sold dried and look like tiny, white beads. When cooked, they become shiny and translucent. Any type of melon can be used — canteloupe or rock melon are just as tasty as the traditional honeydew.

1 ripe honeydew melon
2 cups (500 ml) water
¹/₂ cup (75 g) sago beads
  or tapioca pearls
¹/₂ cup (100 g) sugar
2 cups (500 ml) thick coconut
  milk

1 Halve the honeydew. Using a round melon baller or spoon, scoop out tiny balls of the honeydew flesh. Place the melon balls in a bowl and chill in the refrigerator. Scrape the remaining flesh from the melon and blend in a blender to a smooth puree. Set aside.

2 In a saucepan, bring the water to a boil over high heat. Add the sago beads or tapioca pearls and cook until translucent, about 5 minutes. Reduce the heat to low, add the sugar and stir until the sugar is dissolved. Remove from the heat and set aside to cool. When cool, combine the sago mixture with the coconut milk and the honeydew puree. Chill the dessert in the refrigerator.

3 Spoon the chilled dessert into individual serving bowls, top with honeydew balls and serve with or without ice cubes.

Serves 4 to 6   Preparation time: 20 mins + 2 hours chilling
Cooking time: 10 mins

Sweet Red Bean Pancakes

Although popularly known as a Shanghainese speciality, several provinces including Sichuan make a similar version. Sweetened lotus seed and red bean pastes are both sold ready prepared in cans or plastic packets. If you prefer to make your own lotus seed paste, see the recipe on page 108. These pancakes can be prepared several hours ahead of the meal. Reheat them on both sides on a lightly greased pan just before serving.

½ cup (75 g) flour, sifted and mixed with a pinch of salt

4 tablespoons cornstarch

1 teaspoon custard powder

1 egg

³/₄ cup (185 ml) water

2 tablespoons oil

½ cup (150 g) red bean paste or Sweet Lotus Seed Paste (see page 108)

1 Combine all the ingredients (except the oil and red bean paste or Sweet Lotus Seed Paste) in a mixing bowl, and beat to a smooth batter.

2 Lightly grease a crepe or omelet pan with a bit of oil and heat over low heat until hot. Stir the batter well and ladle ⅓ cup (80 ml) of the batter onto the pan, tilting it from side to side to spread the batter into a thin pancake. Cook the pancake until set, about 1 minute, and remove from the heat. Continue to make 7 more pancakes in this manner or until all the batter is used up.

3 Place the pancakes on a flat surface. Spread 1 tablespoon of the red bean paste or Sweet Lotus Seed Paste evenly on each one, then fold the 4 sides inwards over the filling to form a rectangle, overlapping slightly at the edges.

4 Lightly grease and reheat the same pan over medium heat. Pan-fry the coated pancakes until golden brown and fairly crispy, about 2 minutes on each side. Cut the pancakes into serving pieces and serve hot.

Makes 8 pancakes   **Preparation time: 15 mins**   **Cooking time: 30 mins**

Rice Flour Layered Cakes

The all-time favorite of the Chinese diaspora in Southeast Asia, these cakes are formed by alternating pink and white layers of batter and then adding with a bright red layer on top. The auspicious colors and the layers — representing progress and growth — create the perfect ceremonial confection.

1 cup (250 ml) water

1 cup (250 ml) thick coconut milk

$^3/_4$ cup (150 g) sugar

3 pandanus leaves (or 2 to 3 drops pandanus or rose essence)

$^3/_4$ cup (90 g) long grain rice flour, sifted

$^1/_2$ cup (60 g) tapioca flour, sifted

4 tablespoons mung bean flour, sifted

1 drop pink food coloring

1 round or square steaming tray or cake pan, lightly greased

1 to 2 drops red food coloring

Serves 4 to 6
Preparation time: 20 mins
Cooking time: 1 hour

1 Heat the water, coconut milk, sugar and pandanus leaves or rose essence over low heat in a saucepan, stirring until the sugar is dissolved, about 5 minutes, then simmer for 2 to 3 more minutes to allow the pandanus flavor to be absorbed. Remove from the heat and set aside to cool. Discard the pandanus leaves.

2 Add the cooled coconut syrup to the sifted flours in a mixing bowl and mix well to form a smooth batter, then strain to remove any lumps. Pour 1 cup (250 ml) of the batter into a bowl, add the pink food coloring and mix until well blended. Pour $^1/_4$ cup (60 ml) of the batter into another bowl, add the red food coloring and mix until well blended. Leave the remaining batter as it is.

3 Place the steaming tray or cake pan on a rack in a wok or steamer filled with boiling water, making sure that it is level, cover and heat for 3 minutes. Pour $^1/_4$ cup (60 ml) of the uncolored batter into the tray to form a thin layer. (The batter will spread into a thin layer by itself.) Cover and steam for 1 to 2 minutes until the layer is set. Remove the cover and gently pour $^1/_4$ cup (60 ml) of the pink batter over the first layer. Replace the cover and steam for 3 to 5 minutes until the second layer is set. Repeat to form the third layer with the uncolored batter.

4 Continue the steaming process to alternate white and pink layers (9 layers altogether). Finally make the top bright red layer by pouring the bright red batter over the cake, cover and steam for 15 minutes until cooked. Remove and set aside to cool.

5 Cut the layer cake into diamond shapes or other desired shapes, arrange on a serving platter and serve chilled or at room temperature.

NOTES: Any medium-sized cake pan or heatproof baking dish may be used to steam the cake, as long as it fits inside your wok or steamer and is at least 2 in (6 cm) deep. The illustration at right shows a much larger steaming tray, but this recipe calls for a smaller one — approximately 7 in (18 cm) across. When steaming the layers, constantly stir the uncooked batter to prevent the flour from settling to the bottom. Always wipe the underside of the cover before replacing it on the wok or steamer to prevent water from dropping onto the cake from the lid, as this will make the smooth surface uneven. Constantly top up the water in the wok or steamer with hot water whenever it runs low.

Golden Lotus Seed Pastries

This recipe is a version of *chin tui chai* (in Cantonese), an old traditional favorite that is also a festive confection. Lotus seed paste is an expensive ingredient and is usually reserved for special occasions. On ordinary days, this pastry can be filled with ground peanut, peanut butter or grated coconut cooked in sugar.

10 oz (300 g) sweet potatoes
³/₄ cup (100 g) glutinous rice flour, sifted
2 tablespoons caster sugar
1 cup (10 oz/300 g) Sweet Lotus Seed Paste (see page 108)
8 tablespoons sesame seeds
Oil for deep-frying

1 Prepare the sweet potatoes by peeling them and then boiling or steaming them until cooked. In a mixing bowl, mash the sweet potatoes until smooth, then combine with the flour and sugar, and mix until well blended, adding 2 to 3 tablespoons of water if the sweet potatoes are low in moisture. Flour your hands, gather up the dough and knead until smooth.

2 Lightly dust a flat surface, roll the dough into a cylinder and slice it into 20 equal pieces. Roll each piece into a ball, then flatten it into a thin circle about 3 in (8 cm) in diameter. Place the dough circles on a lightly floured surface or plate and set aside.

3 Lightly wet your hands, spoon 1 heaping teaspoon of the Sweet Lotus Seed Paste and roll it into a ball. Continue to make a total of 20 balls.

4 To wrap the filling with the dough, place a dough circle on your palm and top with a lotus seed ball. Fold the edges of the dough circle around the filling, then seal the edges and roll into a stuffed ball. Continue with the remaining ingredients to make 20 stuffed balls in all.

5 Roll the stuffed balls in a plate of the sesame seeds until well coated on all sides.

6 Heat the oil in a wok over high heat until hot, and deep-fry the coated balls for 3 to 4 minutes, until golden brown and crispy, turning constantly. Place on a serving platter and serve hot or chilled.

Makes 20 pastries   Preparation time: 1 hour   Cooking time: 10 mins

Steamed Rice Flour Cupcakes

A favorite choice for offerings to the gods, these cupcakes are called *fatt ko* in Cantonese, meaning "to prosper."

$^1/_2$ cup (100 g) sugar

1 $^1/_2$ cups (375 ml) water or thin coconut milk

1 to 2 drops rose essence

1 teaspoon sugar

1 $^1/_2$ tablespoons warm water

2 teaspoons instant yeast

2 $^1/_2$ cups (300 g) long grain rice flour, sifted

$^1/_3$ cup (50 g) flour, sifted

1 teaspoon baking powder

1 to 2 drops pink food coloring

4 tablespoons carbonated soda drink (ice cream soda or 7-up)

12 Chinese teacups or cupcake molds

1 Heat the sugar and water or coconut milk in a saucepan over low heat and stir until the sugar is dissolved, 2 to 3 minutes. Stir in the rose essence and remove from the heat. Set aside to cool.

2 In a small bowl, combine the sugar and warm water and mix until the sugar is dissolved. Stir in the yeast and leave the mixture to ferment for about 10 minutes in a warm room until it becomes light and frothy.

3 Place the rice flour in a mixing bowl. Add the cooled syrup and mix well. Fold in the flour and baking powder, and mix until a smooth batter is obtained. Add the pink food coloring and mix until the batter is evenly colored, then stir in the carbonated soda drink and mix until well combined. Add the yeast mixture and stir lightly. Allow the batter to stand in a warm room for 1 $^1/_4$ hours.

4 Lightly grease the teacups or cupcake molds with a little oil and pre-steam them (5 minutes for Chinese teacups or 3 minutes for metal cupcake molds) in a wok (see page 19) or steamer. Fill each teacup or cupcake mold $^3/_4$ full with the batter. Cover the wok or steamer and continue to steam over high heat for about 30 minutes until cooked. Remove from the heat and set aside to cool.

5 Run a knife round the rim of each cake to dislodge before turning them out from the cups or molds. Arrange the cakes on a serving platter and serve at room temperature.

Makes 12 cakes   Preparation time: 30 mins + 1 $^1/_4$ hours for the batter to stand Cooking time: 40 mins

PART TWO
Chinese Festivals

The Chinese celebrate life and all its pleasures in a series of festivals held throughout the year according to the traditional lunar calendar. A few have disappeared with time, but many popular Chinese festivals have endured. Indeed, in difficult times, a festival such as Chinese New Year is all the more important as it offers hope and renewal. The origins of many Chinese festivals can be traced back to as far as the Shang Dynasty (1766-1154 BC). Some appeared much later, during the Ming and Qing Dynasties.

Festivals were always closely linked with agriculture. People worshiped heaven and earth, the moon and stars, mountains and rivers, beseeching these forces to bestow upon them harmonious winds, timely rain, sunshine and bountiful harvests. When their prayers were answered, joyous feasts were held and sacrifices were made to the gods to solicit their continued protection.

The course of social and political development wrought many changes in China. Some festivals lost their original meaning. Others gained new content by way of legends, myths and new beliefs. Through such embellishments, festivals also gained many culinary elements. Some, like the Dragon Boat and Mooncake Festivals, have become major culinary events. Dumplings and mooncakes in dazzling variety and quantity mark their respective seasons. They also make ideal gifts. Sending out gifts of food during festival times is a pleasurable way of renewing and strengthening links, an enduring feature of the Chinese cultural system. Festive concoctions, seasonal delicacies, live poultry, fruit and liquor — all are sent to elders, relatives and friends who have done one a favor or an honor. In Chinese custom, people must return, in one form or other, what has been received before the year is out. For this reason, the tradition of exchanging gifts reaches a climax during the weeks preceding the Chinese New Year.

Money can buy all you need for a festival. Stores are stocked full with dried meats, dried fruits and other exotica for the Chinese New Year. Hotels, restaurants and *dianxin* eateries proclaim their own special creations during the Dragon Boat and Mooncake Festivals. In the market place, enterprising vendors sell everything and anything: rice flour cakes and sweet buns to appease the hungry spirits, vegetarian dishes for devotees to cleanse the body and soul during the Festival of the Nine Emperor Gods, dumplings, mooncakes and *niangao*. It is still de rigueur, however, to share something that you make in your own kitchen. If the fruits of your labor meet with acclaim — such as my mother's dumplings, which always get a round of applause each year — this brings a great satisfaction.

Festival specialities are not easy to prepare. Skill and patience are required to produce good results. This is why many people prefer to buy them. Making your own can, however, be a rewarding experience and, like many other things, practice makes perfect.

The Dragon Boat Festival

In the old days, glutinous rice dumplings were a once-a-year treat. The Chinese made these bamboo leaf-wrapped bundles (called *chung* in the Cantonese-speaking south and *zongzi* in the Mandarin-speaking north) to celebrate the Dragon Boat Festival. Every family had its own special recipe handed down through generations, and everyone made their own *zongzi*. Those who did not depended on the goodwill of friends and relatives for a taste of this popular concoction. Nowadays, one can eat *zongzi* throughout the year at *dianxin* restaurants or buy them from shops and vendors in the marketplace. Nonetheless, come festival times, the rush to order and buy them makes it seem as if people do not get to taste dumplings the rest of the year. Many more people will be making their own, using a well-loved family recipe for this special occasion.

The Dragon Boat Festival falls on the fifth day of the fifth lunar month and is therefore often referred to as the "Double Fifth." Many Chinese simply call it the Fifth Month Festival. Originally, the season was linked to practices aimed at avoiding diseases and calamities during the hot summer months. The Double Fifth marks a change in the weather in China, from a cool spring to a hot, steamy summer. Under such conditions, all creatures, both large and small breed easily — including germs, poisonous snakes, rats and harmful insects. These contribute to calamities and the spread of diseases. To combat this "evil," people would hang calamus weed and mugwort leaves over their doorways and above the head of their bed. They also burned realgar, a reddish mineral with a powerful odor, to ward off insects and other undesirable creatures. Adults drank realgar wine, believed to fortify the body against infection. Or else they bathed in diluted wine water. At festival times, girls carried fragrant pouches and children were given worm powder. The Double Fifth was a time for preventive activities in old China.

It was also the time to propitiate the River God, conceptualized in the form of a dragon. According to ancient beliefs, the dragon ruled the waters and deter-mined the distribution of clouds and rain. The fifth

month precedes the arrival of the summer rains. Floods
ruined crops and livestock. To avert disaster, people offered
sacrifices to the dragon. For their efforts, they hoped to be
favored with a timely and equitable distribution of rainfall
— neither too little nor too much — so that they could reap
bumper harvests. Much depended on the dragon's temper, so
people were very anxious to placate this ruler of the waters.

The preparation and eating of *zongzi* — the custom most
widely associated with the festival today — emerged many
centuries later. It began as a ritual honoring the great poet
and scholar Qu Yuan, who died in 230 BC. The member
of a powerful noble family, Qu Yuan was marked for high
office in the imperial court of Chu. Unwavering loyalty
and a gift for politics earned him the ruler's trust. This was
the period of the Warring States and palace intrigues were
rife. Jealous of the young courtier's growing influence over
the ruler, a group of ambitious, unscrupulous ministers plotted
Qu Yuan's downfall. They succeeded in sowing seeds of
suspicion in the ruler's mind and the poet fell from favor.
Later, when he attacked corrupt practices in the imperial
administration through his poetry, palace ministers joined
forces to have him banished from the court. Dissidents were
not taken lightly in the Middle Kingdom.

In exile, the disillusioned Qu Yuan led a wandering
life south of the Yangzi River. During his travels, he wrote
many outstanding poems. His stirring works on the politics
of his time and his reflections on his country and its woes —
worsening now under the rule of incompetent, pleasure-
seeking officials — are literary masterpieces and have secured
him a prominent place among China's beloved poets.

When the Kingdom of Chu fell — as Qu Yuan had
feared it would — into the hands of the Qin, a state whose

**The rhythmic beating of drums on colorful "dragon boats" during the
annual races now serves to synchronize the rowing of oarsmen, but
also recalls the beating of drums to frighten the fish away from the
poet Qu Yuan when he jumped in the river and drowned.**

hegemonistic ambitions he had repeatedly warned about, he was a broken man. Trapped between enemy territory and the advancing armies of Qin (whose leader was to become the first emperor of China — Shi Huangdi of the terracotta army fame), Qu Yuan wandered aimlessly. On the fifth day of the fifth moon, he came to the Miluo Jiang, a river flowing into the Dongting Lake. Weary and sick at heart at the fate of his beloved country, he sat down and composed a poem — the celebrated Huai Sha — in which he poured out his grief. Then, in despair, he jumped into the river and drowned.

When people heard this, they rushed out in boats to look for him, beating drums and gongs to frighten the fish away from his body. The Chinese always love a poet, and one who lived and died heroically for his country stirs the imagination with the power of romance and melancholy beauty. When the poet's body could not be found, they threw rice-filled bamboo stems into the river to honor his soul. Grandmothers have their own way of telling this story: some say the rice was to feed the creatures in the river so they would not feast on the poet's body. Others maintain it was to feed Qu Yuan's hungry spirit. Whatever the reason, it was the beginning of a custom that survives until today.

Over the course of time, the rice-filled bamboo stems gave way to elaborate preparations and adopted new styles, shapes and content: pyramids bound in bamboo leaves — the most recognizable being lotus leaf "pillows," very popular in Hong Kong — or large banana leaf cones, a style favored by people in Hainan. For as long as anybody can remember, nobody has thrown these into the river. Indeed, dumplings with their fillings of chestnuts, mushrooms and all things nice, are too delicious to throw into the river for the fish to eat. And Qu Yuan is long gone. So the people eat the *zongzi* themselves and hold dragon boat races to commemorate the night that people rowed out in their boats to look for the poet's body.

Stuffed Rice Dumplings

Like so many other recipes, this one has been handed down through the generations of my family, by observing and assisting the older generations go about their tasks in the kitchen. It is important to use pork with enough fat — 5o per cent is just about right — or the dumplings will not be tender or flavorsome. The dumplings can be kept up to a week in the refrigerator or one month in the freezer.

1 $\frac{1}{2}$ cups (3oo g) uncooked glutinous rice, soaked for 5 hours, then drained

$\frac{3}{4}$ cups (125 g) dried red beans, soaked for 5 hours, drained

1 tablespoon salt

4o dried bamboo leaves (see note), soaked overnight, then drained

1o strings, each 6o in (1 $\frac{1}{2}$ m) in length (see page 87)

1o salted preserved egg yolks, halved

2o dried chestnuts, soaked for 3 hours, then drained

4 dried Chinese sausages (*lap cheong*), each cut into 5 pieces

DRIED SHRIMP FILLING

1 $\frac{1}{2}$ tablespoons oil

6 shallots, minced

1 cup (12o g) dried shrimp, soaked for 15 minutes, then rinsed well and drained

$\frac{1}{2}$ teaspoon five spice powder

$\frac{1}{2}$ teaspoon sugar

$\frac{1}{2}$ teaspoon ground white pepper

SEASONED PORK

1 $\frac{1}{2}$ lbs (75o g) pork belly

$\frac{3}{4}$ teaspoon five spice powder

$\frac{1}{2}$ teaspoon ground white pepper

$\frac{3}{4}$ teaspoon salt

1 Prepare the Dried Shrimp Filling first by heating the oil in a wok over medium heat until hot. Stir-fry the minced shallots and dried shrimp until fragrant and crispy, 3 to 5 minutes, seasoning with the five spice powder, sugar and pepper. Remove from the heat and set aside.

2 Make the Seasoned Pork by placing the pork in a heatproof dish and steam it in a covered wok (see page 19) or steamer over high heat for about 2o minutes. Remove from the heat. Drain the pork and slice it into 2o pieces, then season with the five spice powder, pepper and salt.

3 Combine the soaked glutinous rice and red beans in a large mixing bowl, add the salt and mix until well blended. Set aside.

4 To make the dumplings, follow the steps described on page 87. For each dumpling, place 1 tablespoon of the rice and bean mixture into the cone, followed by 1 egg yolk halve, 1 piece of Seasoned Pork, 1 chestnut, 1 piece of sausage and $\frac{1}{2}$ tablespoon of the Dried Shrimp Filling, and cover with 2 more tablespoons of the rice and bean mixture. Use up all the ingredients to make a total of 2o dumplings.

5 Bring a large pot of water to a boil over high heat. Place the dumplings into the pot, making sure they are totally immersed. Return to a boil, cover and boil the dumplings for about 6 hours, adding more boiling water from time to time, until the dumplings are well cooked. Remove from the heat and hang the dumplings up to dry. If the pot is not large enough to fit all the dumplings, boil the dumplings in separate pots.

6 Unwrap the dumplings carefully and serve hot.

NOTES: You can buy dried bamboo leaves and straw for the strings from Chinese grocers. Some supermarkets stock them as well. Buy more than the number required in the recipe to allow for spoilage in the process of wrapping. Before using, soak the dried bamboo leaves and straw overnight to soften, then wash them in clean water and wipe dry with a cloth. To reheat refrigerated dumplings, steam for 15 minutes over high heat or microwave for 2 minutes on high. Reheat frozen dumplings for a longer period; 45 minutes steaming or microwave 3 to 5 minutes.

**Makes 2o dumplings   Preparation time: 2 hours + overnight soaking
Cooking time: 6 hours**

Seasoned Rice Dumplings

Lightly seasoned fried rice is used in this recipe to make a rich, flavorful dumpling — a style favored by the Fukienese. Frying makes the grains sticky and therefore easier to bundle.

15 dried chestnuts

4 dried black Chinese mushrooms

32 dried bamboo leaves (see page 85), soaked overnight, then cleaned and dried

8 strings, each 60 in (1½ m) in length (see page 87)

RICE FILLING

3 tablespoons oil

1½ cups (300 g) uncooked glutinous rice

2 teaspoons salt

4 teaspoons soy sauce

2 teaspoons black soy sauce

½ teaspoon sesame oil

⅓ teaspoon ground white pepper

DRIED SHRIMP FILLING

1 cup (120 g) dried shrimp

1½ tablespoons oil

4 shallots, minced

⅓ teaspoon five spice powder

½ teaspoon sugar

⅓ teaspoon ground white pepper

SEASONED PORK

1 lb (500 g) pork belly

⅔ teaspoon five spice powder

⅓ teaspoon ground white pepper

2 teaspoons salt

1 Prepare the dried ingredients first. Soak the dried chestnuts in water for about 3 hours until soft, then drain. Soak the Chinese mushrooms in hot water for 30 minutes, then drain and squeeze dry. Remove and discard the stems and slice the caps into 15 strips. Soak the glutinous rice in water for about 5 hours, then drain. Soak the dried shrimp in water for about 15 minutes, then rinse in several changes of water and drain. Set all the soaked ingredients aside.

2 To make the Rice Filling, heat 2 tablespoons of the oil in a wok over medium heat until hot. Reduce the heat to low, stir-fry the glutinous rice for 4 to 5 minutes, adding the remaining oil gradually. Season with all the other ingredients and stir-fry for another 3 to 4 minutes until well combined. Remove from the heat and set aside to cool.

3 Prepare the Dried Shrimp Filling and Seasoned Pork by following steps 1 and 2 described on page 85.

4 To make the dumplings, follow the instructions on the opposite page. For each dumpling, place 1 tablespoon of the Rice Filling into the cone, followed by 1 piece of Seasoned Pork, 1 chestnut, 1 mushroom strip, ½ tablespoon of the Dried Shrimp Filling, and cover with 1 more tablespoon of the Rice Filling on top. Use all the ingredients to make a total of 15 or 16 dumplings.

5 Bring a large pot of water to a boil over high heat. Place the dumplings into the pot, making sure they are totally immersed. Return to a boil, cover and boil the dumplings for about 4 hours, adding more boiling water from time to time, until the dumplings are well cooked. Remove from the heat and hang the dumplings up to dry. Serve hot.

Makes 16 dumplings   Preparation time: 1½ hours + overnight soaking
Cooking time: 4 hours

How to Wrap a Rice Dumpling in Bamboo Leaves

There are many ways to wrap rice dumplings. The "triangle" style is by far the most popular. There are actually four points in this bundle and four faces, and each face is triangular in shape, like a pyramid. In skilled hands, each face becomes a perfect triangle.

1 Cut the strings — twine, raffia, kitchen strings or softened straw — into 60 in (1 $\frac{1}{2}$ m) lengths. Lay 5 to 6 strings together and fold them in half, then knot the folded ends together into a loop. Repeat to make enough bundles of strings for the recipe. Hang the bundles of string up and arrange all the ingredients on a table in front of you.

2 Take two bamboo leaves and place them on top of each other lengthwise with the hard rib side facing down so they overlap slightly, offset by about 1 in (2 $\frac{1}{2}$ cm).

3 Fold the leaves around each other in the center to form a wide cone. Hold the cone with one hand and fill it with the ingredients using the other hand, adding the ingredients in sequence as instructed in the recipe. Lightly press the filling with the back of a spoon to pack it down.

4 To wrap the dumpling up, hold the base of the cone tightly with one hand and fold the two leaf ends down over the filling with the other hand, then fold the leaf ends over opposite sides of the cone so they cover the open side of the cone.

5 While still holding the cone with one hand, complete the wrapping by tucking the leaf ends to one side of the cone, forming a tight pyramid.

6 Lift a string from the bundle and wind it tightly twice around the sides of the pyramid, then tie it into a knot to secure.

7 Continue to wrap the other dumplings in this manner until all the strings are used up, forming a bundle of dumplings.

Rice Dumplings with Dark Coconut Syrup

Ideally, these should be small, dainty parcels and should be loosely packed. Alkaline water, a diluted solution of baking soda, plumps up the rice during cooking. The result is a soft, golden dumpling with a light "springy" texture. Be sure to use pure glutinous rice. Any normal rice grains mixed in with it become hard and speckled. The dumplings themselves are not sweet, but when the soft, springy bundles are eaten with a sweet sauce, they are a delight to the senses. They can be served with honey, maple or golden syrup, but my own favorite is a dark syrup of molasses and coconut milk. I like it chilled, but it is equally delicious served warm.

2 $\frac{1}{2}$ cups (500 g) uncooked pure glutinous rice

1 $\frac{1}{2}$ teaspoons alkaline water or baking soda solution (see page 138)

60 to 70 dried bamboo leaves (see page 85), soaked overnight to soften, cleaned and dried

15 strings, each 60 in (1 $\frac{1}{2}$ m) in length (see page 87)

DARK COCONUT SYRUP

$\frac{1}{2}$ cup (125 ml) mild molasses

$\frac{1}{2}$ cup (125 ml) water

2 tablespoons sugar

$\frac{1}{2}$ cup (125 ml) thick coconut milk

1 Soak the glutinous rice in water for about 5 hours until soft, then drain. Add the alkaline water to the soaked glutinous rice, a little at a time and mix until well combined. Set aside for 4 to 5 hours.

2 Fill and wrap the dumplings as described on page 87. Use about 2 tablespoons of the soaked glutinous rice to fill each dumpling.

3 Cook the dumplings for 6 hours as described on page 85.

4 While boiling the dumplings, prepare the Dark Coconut Syrup by heating the molasses, water and sugar over low heat in a small saucepan, stirring occasionally, until the sugar is dissolved and the mixture thickens into a syrup, about 5 minutes. Stir in the coconut milk and simmer for a further 4 to 5 minutes. Remove from the heat and transfer to a serving bowl.

5 Serve the dumplings hot or chilled with Dark Coconut Syrup, or with any other type of syrup or honey.

Makes 25 to 30 dumplings
Preparation time: 1 $\frac{1}{2}$ hours + overnight soaking
Cooking time: 6 hours

Salted Preserved Eggs

Salted egg yolks have a wonderful flavor and texture. Every connoisseur knows they add
a touch of luxury to rice dumplings (*zongzi*). Salted preserved eggs can be bought from
Chinese grocers. Unlike the century eggs which are coated with a layer of brown wood ash,
these eggs are instantly recognizable by their black protective covering — a mixture of ash
and clay. Remove this layer and rinse well before breaking the eggs. Chicken eggs can be used,
but duck eggs have a better flavor. For *zongzi* and other recipes in this book,
only the solid egg yolk is used. Discard the runny whites.

1 cup (300 g) coarse sea salt

1 tablespoon peppercorns

6 cups (1 1/2 liters) water

2 tablespoons rice wine

10 duck or chicken eggs, cleaned

1 Combine the salt, peppercorns, water and rice wine in a large pot. Heat over very low heat, stirring constantly, until the salt is completely dissolved, 5 to 10 minutes. Remove and set aside to cool.

2 When cooled, pour the brine into a clean, non-metallic jar (a glass, ceramic or earthenware jar). Carefully lower the eggs into the brine, making sure that all the eggs are totally immersed. Cover the jar and leave at room temperature for 30 days.

3 After 30 days, the salted preserved eggs are ready to be used. Remove the eggs from the jar and dry them on a rack. Store the dried eggs in a cool, dry place.

Makes 10 eggs   **Preparation time: 5 mins**   **Cooking time: 10 mins**

The Hungry Ghost Festival

They are always hungry, trapped in a hellish realm where nothing can reach them. They are "hungry ghosts," forms whose throats are constricted as if they were hung upside down. In the cycle of karma, people who have indulged in excesses are reborn into this realm when they die. Here they are denied the cycle of birth, life and death, and are imprisoned for eternity.

Once a year they are allowed a respite. According to Chinese belief, the gates of Hell open on the first day of the seventh lunar month, and for thirty days the hungry spirits are free to roam the earth and mingle with human beings. Clearly, such an occurance makes everybody uncomfortable, particularly when these demons are believed to possess awesome powers of destruction. To keep peace and harmony between themselves and the hungry ghosts – co-existence being preferred to conflict – the Chinese go to great lengths to appease the spirits. Food, drink, entertainment and money are provided in ceremonies held throughout the month. Contented spirits, it is assumed, are like contented people. They will not make trouble. Nevertheless, joyful events such as marriages and celebrations of good fortune are traditionally avoided in the seventh month as it would be foolhardy to tempt the demons.

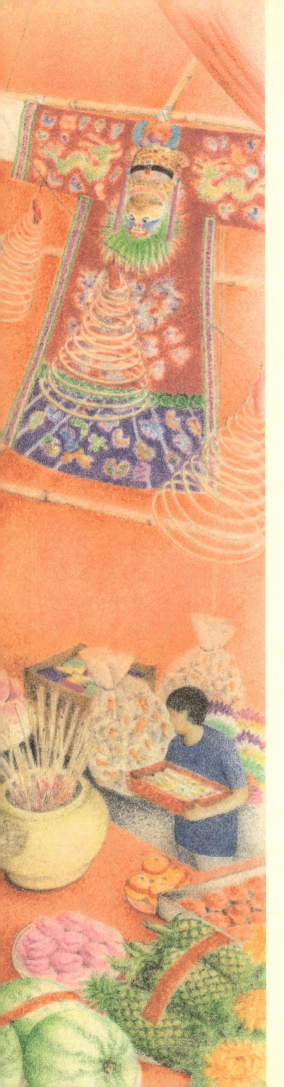

Like all Chinese festivals, the celebration of the seventh month was associated in earlier times with a period in the agricultural cycle — in this case the harvest time (when food was relatively plentiful). With the introduction of Buddhist elements in the third century, this simple offering festival evolved into an event filled with color and spectacle. Central to this complex system of folk beliefs, rituals and celebrations is the salvation of the destitute.

Chinese Buddhists believe they can be saved by the power of mass prayer. This belief owes its origin to the story of Mu Lian, a monk who rescued his mother from Hell. A disciple of Buddha, Mu Lian had attained powers which enabled him to traverse the cosmos. One day, during an experiment, he was horrified to find his mother, who had committed great evil in her life, imprisoned in the terrible dungeons of the underworld. Mu Lian tried to get her out but failed. He brought her nourishment and clothing, but everything she touched turned to fire. Desperate, Mu Lian appealed to the Buddha for help.

The Buddha said that he alone could not save his disciple's mother. She could only be saved by the power of joy, a colossal vortex which required the collective power of a gathering of the Bodhisattvas or "enlightened" ones — pure in spirit, boundless in magnanimity, joyful in harmony — through recitations at the hour of supreme cosmic bliss. Before this, Mu Lian was to initiate certain rituals to link the proceedings to his mother, beginning with the worship of his ancestors going back seven generations. When all instructions had been faithfully carried out, Mu Lian set about preparing a great feast for the gathering. On the fifteenth day of the ritual seventh lunar month, at the hour when form and formlessness were in blissful harmony, the Buddha and a hundred of his disciples gathered to perform the feat.

A communal "party" for the wandering hungry ghosts is a time for lavish offerings of food and entertainment that was traditionally held around the harvest time in ancient China.

93

The happy ending and the element of filial piety of the story appeals greatly to the Chinese — Taoists as well as Buddhists — and to this day similar rituals are performed during the seventh month. The aim is to ease the suffering of the hungry ghosts and, more importantly, to exonerate the spirits. The accomplishments of Mu Lian illuminated the way whereby the fortunate may enter the virtuous cycle of life, death and rebirth, the only escape from the realm of the hungry ghosts.

But it is the less enlightened and those worshiping out of fear, who are more concerned with their own safety and well-being than the plight of the hungry ghosts, who bring color and excitement to this festival. Individual households observe the tradition of appeasement on the fourteenth or fifteenth day of the month. On this day, as is the tradition in all Chinese festivals, the ancestors and household gods are nourished and worshiped. Afterwards, the family feasts and makes merry. Come nightfall, upon the hour of ghostly pursuits (spirits are perceived to be nocturnal), food and the paraphernalia of worship are carried outside the house. The ceremony takes place in the house compound or on the street if one lives in a highrise in the city. Burning joss sticks and candles, the lady of the house invites the spirits to help themselves to the food spread out on the ground. When the starved spirits have stuffed themselves (good manners and refinement are not expected of the hungry ghosts), an assortment of brightly-colored paper treasures assembled from joss papers is burned. Included will be bags of money in gold and silver in the form of shoe-shaped ingots, folded from joss papers, to simulate ancient currency. Ghosts need money to pursue pleasure or grease the palms of those who stand in their way. To the Chinese mind, greed and corruption know no boundaries.

This festival is celebrated throughout the month by Chinese from different precincts, clan houses or trade houses. Each community chooses its own timetable. It is always a grand affair. Magnificent tableaus of the King of the Hungry Ghosts and his council in all their paper splendor are set up in the marketplace, clan house or under huge canopies in the street. The party mood is set when huge flags are posted by the side of the street leading to the tableau. The event may last from two to seven days, depending on the funds raised by the organizers.

At noon on the first day, a Taoist priest is invited to perform the initiation rites. He paints the "breath of life" into the paper effigies, which are considered inanimate until anointed with a spot of vermilion ink on various parts of the face and body, the eyes, ears, nose, nostrils, mouth, hands, feet and navel. This done, the King of the Hungry Ghosts and the members of his council come alive. For the protection of man, it is important to keep this distinguished company in good spirits. They are the enforcers of law, with the power to incarcerate the rest of the population of their kind should they prove too unruly.

Food and drink, enough to satisfy the most monstrous appetites, are piled before this awesome group: wheat buns heaped into pyramids, stacks of rice cakes, mountains of fruit, chickens, ducks, and whole roast pigs. Entertainment is provided while the spectral beings enjoy their feast. A traditional Chinese opera is a sure winner. Puppet shows were once the rage. Nowadays, many organizers perceive a change in ghostly tastes and a modern pop music program featuring young girls in miniskirts is often staged.

Members of the community arrive at different times during the revelry to offer food, drinks or presents. They also watch the shows. But out of respect, or perhaps fear, the front row of seats is left unoccupied. These are reserved for the King of the Hungry Ghosts and his retinue.

The party ends at midnight on the last day with a spectacular ceremonial fire in which all the splendid paper effigies together with the ornate robes, flags and paper treasures in the brilliant colors of the rainbow, bags of gold and silver "money" to buy protection or favor — go up in flames. Presumably, the ghosts are satisfied with the participants for a task well done, and in a mutual understanding that has stood the test of time, they will now return contentedly to where they belong or leave the vicinity, making it safe once more.

Steamed Fortune Buns

Stacks of these bright pink buns are offered to the King of the Hungry Ghosts and his retinue as part of the appeasement ceremony. The buns are then divided among members of the community who have sponsored the event. Fortune buns, or *mee koo* (in Hokkien), were originally made to celebrate birthdays and distributed to well-wishers. *Mee koo* means "bread tortoise" since the buns are shaped to resemble the tortoise, a symbol of longevity. The "shell" is frequently trimmed with strips of colored dough. *Mee Koo* taste best straight from the steamer when they are soft and moist. They are equally good with or without butter.

2 teaspoons sugar

1 $^1/_2$ tablespoons warm water

1 teaspoon instant yeast

$^1/_2$ cup (125 ml) water

$^1/_4$ cup (50 g) sugar

1 $^3/_4$ cups (250 g) flour,
   sifted with $^1/_4$ teaspoon salt

2 teaspoons shortening

$^1/_4$ teaspoon pink food coloring

$^1/_2$ teaspoon baking powder

$^1/_2$ teaspoon baking soda

2 rectangular sheets of baking
   paper (6 x 4 in/ 15 x 10 cm)

Makes 2 buns
Preparation time: 1 hour + 2 hours for
   the dough to stand
Cooking time: 20 mins

1 In a small bowl, combine the sugar and warm water and stir until the sugar is dissolved, then stir in the yeast and leave the mixture to ferment for 5 to 10 minutes in a warm room, or until light and frothy.
2 Bring the water to a boil in a small saucepan. Add the sugar and stir until the sugar is dissolved, 1 to 2 minutes. Remove and set aside to cool.
3 Place the flour in a mixing bowl, stir in the shortening with a fork until well blended. Combine the yeast mixture with the cooled syrup and mix well. Make a well in the center of the flour mixture and gradually pour in the yeast syrup, mixing well with your hands until the flour paste leaves the sides of the bowl to form a dough. On a lightly floured surface, knead the dough until smooth and pliable. Pull out a small piece of dough the size of an egg and place it in a separate bowl. Add the pink food coloring and knead until it is evenly colored. Cover both the pink and uncolored doughs with a cloth and leave them to rise for 1 to 1 $^1/_2$ hours in a warm room or until the dough has doubled in size.
4 Punch down the uncolored dough to release the air. Add the baking powder and baking soda and knead for about 10 minutes to combine. Cover the dough with a cloth and set aside for 30 minutes to rise again.
5 Divide the uncolored dough into 2 equal portions. Flour your hands and shape each portion into an oval-shaped loaf. Divide the pink dough in the same manner and using a rolling pin, roll each portion out into a thin ($^1/_8$ in/2 mm) oval sheet, large enough to cover each dough loaf.
6 Place a pink dough sheet over each uncolored loaf, pressing the top lightly to stick the pink sheet onto the loaf. Turn the loaf over and fold the pink dough sheet inwards all around the base of the loaf, pressing down to seal. Repeat to wrap the remaining dough.
7 Place each wrapped loaf on a sheet of baking paper and brush a little oil over the top of the loaves. Arrange them on a steaming tray and steam in a covered wok (see page 19) or steamer over high heat for 20 minutes. Remove the buns from the heat and serve warm.

Festive Rice Flour Cakes

In presenting ceremonial offerings, you cannot go wrong with rice flour cakes. The gods and ghosts love them. The cakes may be left plain or stained with several colors to dazzle the spirits.

$^3/_4$ cup (150 g) sugar

$1^1/_2$ cups (375 ml) water

2 to 3 drops rose essence

$1^1/_4$ cups (150 g) long grain rice
   flour, sifted

2 tablespoons sugar

2 tablespoons warm water

1 teaspoon instant yeast

1 round or square cake pan, 8 in
   (20 cm) across, lightly greased

1 tablespoon each of pink, yellow
   and green food coloring
   (optional)

Serves 6
Preparation time: 20 mins + 2 hours for
   the dough to stand
Cooking time: 30 mins

1 Heat the sugar and $^3/_4$ cup (185 ml) of the water over low heat in a small saucepan and stir until the sugar is dissolved, 5 to 10 minutes. Remove from the heat, add the rose essence, mix well and set aside to cool.

2 Mix the rice flour and $^1/_2$ cup (125 ml) of the water in a mixing bowl, and knead to form a smooth dough. Pull out a small portion of the dough (about 1 tablespoon/30 g) and place it in a small saucepan with the remaining $^1/_4$ cup (60 ml) of water. Heat the mixture over low heat, stirring constantly until a smooth and starchy paste is obtained, 3 to 4 minutes. Remove from the heat and set aside to cool. Mix the cooled starchy paste with the uncooked dough until smooth. Set aside.

3 In a small bowl, combine the sugar and warm water, and mix until the sugar is dissolved. Stir in the yeast and leave the mixture to ferment for 5 to 10 minutes in a warm room, or until light and frothy. Add the yeast mixture to the soft dough, mix well, and set aside to rise in a warm room for $1^1/_2$ to 2 hours, then add the cooled syrup to the proven dough and mix until a smooth batter is obtained.

4 Place the empty cake pan on a rack in a wok or steamer and steam it for about 5 minutes. With the pan still in the wok or steamer, pour in the batter and get ready to color the batter. Place the various colors of food coloring in separate cups. Dip a fork into the first color, then dip the stained ends of the fork into one spot of the batter, right to the bottom of the tray, to color that spot. Repeat to make 12 to 14 spots of that color at various places in the batter. Separately apply the other two colors in the same way, spacing the colors apart. To create splashes of colors on the cake when cooked, spread the spots of colors by gently swirling them around with a cocktail stick. Cover and steam the pan over high heat for 20 minutes until cooked. Test by inserting the tip of a knife into the center of the cake. When the cake is cooked, the knife should come out cleanly when removed. Remove and set aside to cool.

5 Cut the rice cake into diamond-shaped pieces and serve immediately.

NOTE: It is important to add the food colorings while heating the batter, as hot batter holds the colors within the cake, resulting in a beautiful coloring effect on the cake after steaming.

The Mooncake Festival

Before scientific exploration scaled the heavens and disappointed romantics with some of its discoveries, the moon enjoyed more esoteric connotations — it was the domain of a goddess, a playground for fairies, and the embodiment of all that was feminine. For a greater part of the last millennia, it was inconceivable that the moon was just a space rock.

The Chinese have had a long-standing love affair with the moon that goes as far back as the **H**an **D**ynasty. The crescent disk cycles, proven useful in the development of the calendar, seduced early moon-gazers. **B**ut the **C**hinese reserve songs of praise and acts of worship for the fully round, luminous beauty whose attributes they associate with feminine virtues. **R**igorous and long-standing observation found the moon to be at its most exquisite in mid-autumn, during the eight lunar month.

To salute this eighth month perfection, the great **H**an emperor, **W**udi, initiated a celebration: a banquet followed by a night of "lunar contemplation" when the emperor and his court adjourned to "**T**oad **T**errace" to view the moon and take pleasure in the beauty of the night. **T**oad **T**errace was so named after a popular moon fable, which tells of an angry husband pursuing his terrified wife, **C**hang **E**, across the sky for taking a pill of immortality that was given to him as a reward for his archery skills. **O**n reaching the safety of the moon, **C**hang **E**, out of breath,

spat out the casing of the pill. It instantly turned into a jade rabbit and the lady herself changed into a three-legged toad. Her disappointed husband had to content himself with an abode in the sun, and a meeting between the two on the fifteenth day of every month.

During the *Song Dynasty*, "lunar contemplation" on the fifteenth night of the eighth month gained momentum when the ruling classes began to observe the ritual. Cakes, round like the moon, were prepared to mark the occasion. Exchanging gifts prior to lunar parties also became fashionable. But, the night belonged to the men.

In its early days, "lunar contemplation" was a cerebral affair — the monopoly of the nobility and men of high rank. On this lovely autumn night, the high and the mighty gathered at the great houses to salute the heavenly body and marvel at the splendor of its luminous tranquillity. Luxuriating in surroundings of gilded terraces, silken finery and fragrant gardens, the men drank wine, composed poems, engaged in conversation, contemplated and expanded their visionary pursuits true to the spirit of "lunar contemplation" or *siong yuit*, as the Cantonese describe it, designed to inspire noble and praiseworthy thoughts.

In time, the celebration was adopted by the common people and gained widespread appeal. The wealthy favored parties on board riverboats, or on pavilions erected by a stream or pond, both perfect spots to sight the moon — a breathtaking picture in the still waters, among water lilies, darting fish and graceful willows.

Poets and scholars were much in demand at these parties. They were the glitterati of the time. When the renowned and esteemed were among his guests, a generous host would open his grounds to the common folk, and they would come in droves, observing the evening's entertainment from the

The Mooncake Festival is a time for eating mooncakes and playing out-of-doors with brightly-colored paper lanterns under the glow of a glorious full moon.

periphery of the pavilion. The sight of a poet illuminated by moonlight, reciting poems or singing songs to the gentle strains of the lute, was pure enchantment for these simple folk.

The moonlight festivities became so widespread that they forced some adjustments to the calendar date. Three nights were set aside for "lunar contemplation," justified by an irresistible logic: one night was needed to welcome the goddess (the fourteenth), one night to salute her (the fifteenth), and one night to bid her farewell (the sixteenth). Celebrations could be held on any one of these nights, or on all three. It was a happy arrangement for people who had to fulfill both family and social engagements.

For the ordinary family, the appointment with the goddess was invariably fixed on the fifteenth night, and though short on poetry and splendor, was nevertheless an eagerly awaited event. Everyone would be outdoors — three generations sitting in the moonlight enjoying the fine autumn weather was the norm. Four generation households were even more fortunate. Even today, when the Chinese family gets together, more is definitely merrier.

A table of offerings is set up under the watchful eyes of the goddess. Following a custom set generations before them, the womenfolk line up to pay homage. Joss sticks poised in their clasped hands, a moment of respectful silence or prayer is followed by a kowtow before the joss sticks are secured in the urn, filled with ashes or sometimes sand. The goddess is sure to be in a benevolent mood and so it is an opportune time to make a wish or ask for her blessings.

The rest of the night is devoted to "lunar contemplation." For the ordinary family, this is nothing more than a celebration of simple pleasures in the romantic moonlight, such as marvelling at the beauty of the moon, savoring the delicacies of the season, reminiscing about old times and telling stories. Old "moon stories" are retold and new ones invented. Every good storyteller gives a new twist to an old tale, which explains why there are so many versions of the same story today.

The younger generation, who have been waiting impatiently for the evening to arrive, dreaming of play and all the treats in store, are dressed for the occasion in their best clothes or in new, gaily-colored pajamas. For amusement, they are given lanterns to play with — brightly-colored paper-and-wire contraptions suspended from short bamboo rods. Even tiny tots have no trouble carrying these.

In earlier times, lanterns were mounted on top of long bamboo poles and held up high above the head, like flags. The lanterns were almost always in the shape of animals: fish, birds, rabbits, horses, butterflies, roosters, ducks, dragons and phoenixes. Like everything else, however, lanterns reflect the times. It is not at all surprising nowadays to find Mickey Mouse or some popular comic book hero sneaking into this menagerie for some fun. When man ventured into space, rockets and spaceships cavorted alongside tigers and hummingbirds.

Virtually every child would have a lantern on this night. They would charge around the compound or parade in the street in large groups, singing songs and chanting rhymes. Each proudly bore his treasured possession, illuminated by a candle setting it aglow in the moonlight. Accidents often happened. Occasionally, a lantern would go up in flames before the fun and games were over, ruining the night for the unlucky owner.

In between play, treats awaited the weary. Tired children would hang up their lanterns at any convenient spot, a low branch or the laundry line, and join their elders to listen to "moon stories" and to eat. The tables would overflow with nuts and fruit, boiled water calthrop (*lengkok* in Cantonese — young children have an endless fascination for this bizarre-looking nut, or maybe a legume, that resembles a bird in flight), baby taros, taro pudding and mooncakes in the shape of fish, rabbits and grotesque lions; little piggy

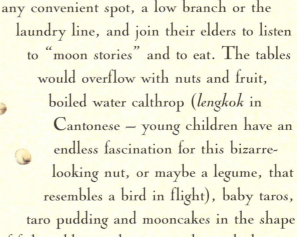

moncakes trapped in miniature hog baskets; round mooncakes with assorted centers of sweetened lotus seed paste, almonds, orange peel, walnuts, bits of ham and yolk of salted duck's eggs.

The original mooncakes were not as picturesque as they are today. People began with plain flour, shaping them round to represent the object of their desire, the moon — never suspecting that these innocuous-looking pastries would one day be instrumental in the fall of an empire.

During the time of the Mongols, China was ruled by a warrior tribe from the Asian steppes who conquered China and set up the Yuan Dynasty. The Han Chinese majority regarded their new rulers with characteristic suspicion. Suspicion turned to hatred when the Mongols began a reign of terror. The Han were subjected to the harshest laws, and rebellion simmered. Secret societies were formed to recruit rebels. The revolutionary forces grew rapidly in number. Military success, however, did not match the rebels' aspirations. Uprisings were quickly quashed. Undeterred, General Zhu Yuanzhang, leader of the rebel army, vowed to continue the struggle and to "crush the Tazis (Tartars)." When the rebels finally achieved victory in a lightly defended district in Anhui Province, the elated general set his next target: the capture of Suzhou, the capital city. For this, the residents had to be exhorted to support the revolutionary forces. This was crucial to their success. But how could they reach the people inside the city? The Mongols kept tight surveillance. Gatherings were forbidden and there was a curfew after dark. It was the eighth month; an idea began to germinate. The rebel general and his military advisers came up with a daring plan: secret messages would be sent into the city using mooncakes. Slips of paper bearing instructions were rolled in waxed paper and inserted into the mooncakes and sent into the city. The unsuspecting Mongols did not make anything of it as it was customary among the Han to send gifts prior to any festival.

At the appointed hour, the revolutionary forces surrounded the city and the people within the walls attacked the Mongols, who were taken completely by surprise. The victory spelled the beginning of the end for the Yuan and marked the rise of the Ming Dynasty. General Zhu became its founding emperor. The role that mooncakes played in this historic battle quickly became known throughout the Middle Kingdom. It was the stuff of legends, and in no time tales were spun of its glory. New styles of mooncakes also evolved. The plain wheat flour pastries took on fancy shapes — of mythical beasts, fish, rabbits and other animals, goddesses and buddhas. These are the picture pastries (*kong chai paeng* in Cantonese), which children love so much. The traditional round cakes with assorted sweet centers that older folk prefer, became more and more fascinating as new varieties developed. Nuts, seeds and citrus peel filled the popular concoctions. Each province had its own distinctive style, but the southern style, categorized as Guangdong pastries and shaped from intricately carved wooden molds, became by far the most popular. Lotus seed paste filled with the bright red yolk of salted preserved eggs encased in a biscuit pastry is the region's premier invention. The Chinese simply love the richness of this unusual combination.

Despite its overtones of war, weapons and battle cries, the Mooncake Festival is essentially a celebration of romance and beauty. Unfortunately, not many Chinese realize this today. Political, social and economic developments have exacted a toll. The venue, too, is changing. Smaller houses and families see fewer household offerings. Instead, people go out. Family groups head for the beach, a hill site, the clan house or simply the suburban park around the corner, children with their lanterns, the elders with their supply of mooncakes, tea and all. The gatherings take place in less formal circumstances. The goddess is an old friend. Ceremonial greetings need not be so elaborate and for some are not even necessary. Familiarity has reduced the moon's mystique. But her enduring beauty will continue to win admirers on this autumn night when the Chinese gather to observe the age-old tradition of "lunar contemplation."

Lotus Seed Mooncakes

Intricately carved wooden molds are used to shape these mooncakes with assorted fillings. There is a great variety of fillings to choose from, and with every autumn more creations are added to the already long list. Sweetened lotus seed filling (*lianrong*) is a classic favorite. Traditionalists love the rich flavor of *lianrong* with a whole yolk of a salted preserved egg in the middle. This may sound strange to the uninitiated but for aficionados, it is a delightful combination. Ready-to-use sweetened lotus seed paste is widely available at this time of the year, as are salted preserved eggs. If you have the time, you may like to try making your own salted preserved eggs — the recipe is given on page 89.

$^1/_2$ cup (125 ml) **Golden Syrup**

2 cups (300 g) **flour**, sifted

1 teaspoon **baking soda**

$^1/_2$ cup (125 ml) **oil**

1 teaspoon **alkaline water** or baking soda solution (see page 134)

$1^1/_2$ cups (1 lb/450 g) **Sweet Lotus Seed Paste** (see below)

10 **salted preserved egg yolks** (optional)

1 **mooncake mold**, $2^1/_2$ in (6 cm) in diameter

1 **egg yolk**, beaten, for brushing

SWEET LOTUS SEED PASTE

$2^1/_2$ cups (150 g) **skinned dried lotus seeds**, soaked in water for 1 hour

$^1/_2$ cup (150 ml) **oil**

$^3/_4$ cup (150 g) **sugar**

1 teaspoon **maltose syrup**

Makes 10 mooncakes

Preparation time: 2 hours + 4 hours for the dough to stand

Cooking time: 25 mins per batch

1 Prepare the Golden Syrup by following the recipe on page 110.

2 Make the Sweet Lotus Seed Paste by boiling the lotus seeds in a pot of water over medium heat until soft, about 1 hour, then draining and grinding them to a smooth paste in a blender. Heat $2^1/_2$ tablespoons of the oil in a non-stick wok or saucepan over high heat. Add 2 tablespoons of the sugar and stir until the mixture caramelizes, 2 to 3 minutes. Reduce the heat to medium, add the lotus seed paste and mix well. Stir in the remaining sugar and mix until the sugar is dissolved. Gradually add the remaining oil and stir until the mixture is thick and pulls away from the sides of the pan, 20 to 30 minutes. Finally stir in the maltose syrup and remove from the heat. Cool the paste overnight before using. This makes about $1^1/_2$ cups (1 lb/450 g) of Sweet Lotus Seed Paste.

3 To make the mooncake dough, combine the flour and baking soda in a mixing bowl. Make a well in the center and gradually stir in the Golden Syrup, oil and alkaline water (or baking soda solution), mixing well with a wooden spoon. Flour you hands and knead the mixture into a smooth dough. Cover with a cloth and set aside for 3 to 4 hours.

4 Once the dough and Sweet Lotus Seed Paste are ready, divide the Sweet Lotus Seed Paste into 10 equal portions, and then roll each portion into a ball between your palms. If using preserved egg yolks, press each paste ball with your thumb to make a depression, then insert a yolk and gather the edges of the paste around the yolk to enclose it.

5 On a floured surface, divide the dough into 10 equal portions and roll each portion into a ball in a similar fashion. Follow the instructions on page 110 to shape the dough and fill each mooncake. Repeat until all the 10 mooncakes have been formed.

6 Bake the cakes in a preheated oven at 400°F (200°C) for about 15 minutes. Remove and brush the top of the cakes with the beaten egg. Return the cakes to bake for 6 to 8 more minutes or until golden brown.

7 To allow the pastry to mellow and taste better, leave the cakes to cool uncovered in a well-ventilated place for 1 to 2 days before eating.

1

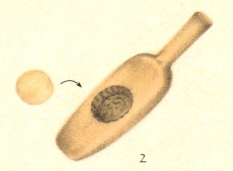

2

3

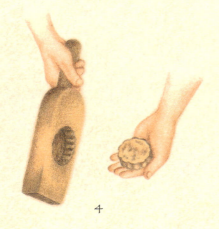

4

NOTE: If you don't have a mooncake mold, shape each filled mooncake into a large round disk. Then using the back of a knife, press groves 1 in (2 ½ cm) apart all around the sides of the cake to make the "pie crust pattern."

How to Shape a Mooncake

1 Once the Sweet Lotus Seed Paste balls have been filled with the egg yolks, and the dough balls have been formed (see pages 108 and 111), flatten one of the dough balls with your palm, then roll it into a ⅛-in (3-mm) thick dough circle using a rolling pin. Hold the dough circle in your palm, place a Sweet Lotus Seed Paste ball in the center and fold the sides of the dough circle around it to completely enclose the lotus paste ball, pressing the edges to seal it.

2 Lightly flour the inside of the mooncake mold, and then press the combined dough ball with the lotus paste filling, seam side up, into the mold.

3 Flatten the dough with your palm so the mooncake conforms to the shape of the mold.

4 Turn the mold over and tap the end of the mold gently on the work surface to dislodge the cake.

Golden Syrup

Prepare the Golden Syrup at least 2 to 3 weeks in advance for the best results. It turns dark and gives a nice golden brown sheen to the mooncakes.

1 ¼ cups (250 g) sugar
¾ cups (185 ml) water
Juice and the rind of ¼ lemon

NOTE: If preferred, you can buy ready-made golden syrup from the supermarket.

1 Bring all the ingredients to a boil over medium heat in a saucepan, stirring until the sugar is dissolved. Reduce the heat to very low and simmer without stirring for 1 to 2 hours, until the mixture caramelizes and turns golden brown, has a consistency like honey, and reduces to about 1 cup (250 ml). Remove from the heat and set aside to cool.

2 Pour the syrup into a covered glass or ceramic jar with an airtight cover and store in a cool, dry place until ready to use. It will keep for several months.

Makes 1 cup (250 ml)   Preparation time: 5 mins   Cooking time: 2 hours

Picture Pastries

These pastries (*kong chai paeng* in Cantonese) with their intriguing forms depicting animals, goddesses and sages appeal mostly to children. Specially carved wooden molds are used to create the various shapes. If these molds are not available, you may use cookie or jelly molds instead. Mooncake pastries are often quite hard when they leave the oven. The standard practice is to allow 3 to 4 days for the golden syrup to mature and soften the pastry.

1 cup (250 ml) **Golden Syrup** (see facing page)

4 cups (600 g) flour, sifted

1 teaspoon baking soda

1 cup (250 ml) oil

1 tablespoon alkaline water or baking soda solution (see page 138)

Mooncake animal molds or shallow jelly molds

1 egg yolk, beaten, for brushing

1 Prepare the Golden Syrup by following the recipe on facing page.

2 Combine the flour and baking soda in a mixing bowl. Make a well in the center and gradually stir in the Golden Syrup, oil and alkaline water (or baking soda solution), mixing well with a wooden spoon. Flour you hands and knead the mixture into a smooth dough. Cover the dough with a cloth and set aside for 3 to 4 hours.

3 On a lightly floured surface, divide the dough into 10 to 20 equal portions, depending on the size of your mold. Shape each cake using the mooncake molds as instructed on facing page. Place the cakes on a lightly greased baking tray.

4 Bake the cakes in a preheated oven at 400°F (200°C) for about 15 minutes. Remove and brush the top of the cakes with the beaten egg. Return the cakes to bake for another 6 to 8 minutes or until golden brown.

5 Leave the cakes to cool uncovered in a well-ventilated place for 3 to 4 days before eating.

Makes 10 to 20 cakes **Preparation time: 20 mins** **Cooking time: 25 mins**

The Winter Solstice Festival

Autumn has passed and the harvest is complete. Sowing will begin when spring comes. In between, there is a long, cold winter and for the predominantly agricultural society in old China, a time of idleness. To brighten up the wintry days, to bring cheer to a bored household, the Chinese invented yet another festival — the last party of the year.

The Winter Festival or Dongzhi falls on the twelfth day of the eleventh lunar month. It coincides with the Winter Solstice when the sun is at its southernmost point above the Tropic of Capricorn — two or three days before Christmas and ten days before the New Year in the Gregorian calendar. This festival marks the turning point between winter and spring, daylight and darkness. Days begin to gain hours as the sun retraces its path northwards. To yesterday's farmers, it is as good as any timetable. They know the winter is halfway over and they will have to start preparing for the coming year's planting once the festivities are over.

The Dongzhi festivities are a departure from the characteristic spectacle and drama that make Chinese festivals so memorable. There are no "ghosts" to contend with, no prancing lions a-calling, only gods and ancestors to appease with copious feasting. To celebrate the completion of the cycle, to make the intangible tangible, everyone eats *tangyuan*, rice flour balls in soup.

The name *tangyuan* suggests unity, perfection and completeness, all very desirable qualities. *Tangyuan* can be sweet boiled in a light syrup, or savory served in a meat and vegetable broth. It is not certain which the gods prefer, so some people, notably the Cantonese, prepare both to play safe.

In today's kitchens, this festive speciality can be whipped up in a couple of hours. The same was not true in the past. Every step was time-consuming and laborious and kept a household busy for many days. Instead of ready-to-use rice flour, grains had to be soaked in basins for an interminable period until ready to be ground into a paste by hand. An old-fashioned, hand-powered grinding stone was used for the job, slowly and surely. The ground rice paste was subsequently put into cloth bags and hung up to drain off the excess liquid. The entire operation had to be timed perfectly so that the ground rice

could be kneaded into a pliable dough and yet remained fresh enough for the rolling of the *tangyuan* on the eve of the festival.

There was never any shortage of willing hands for this ritual, given the size of Chinese families in those times. Children could be counted on and in fact often monopolized the production line: an assembly of older children and tiny tots, their busy palms rolling small pieces of dough into perfect rounds, filling up the trays with neat straight rows or, according to flights of fancy, criss-crosses, grids or sunbursts. Fun and contest clashed constantly with efficiency. Territorial claims and rivalries often ended in flattened balls and squabbles. Once cooked, nobody recognized his or her own handiwork anymore and ownership claims ceased. But for the night, the hand-rolled "marbles" remained a child's pride and joy.

Everyone begins the festival day with a bowl of *tangyuan* for luck, and it is eaten throughout the day until the pot is empty. Ancestors and household gods have their ceremonial fill, in addition to the traditional offering when the feast is prepared. Ancestors who reside in the clan houses (*kongsi* in Cantonese) can expect supplication from the faithful. Dongzhi is one of the three festivals when the ancestors (*pak kung* in Cantonese) in the clan houses are worshiped as well, the other two being during the All Souls Festival (Qingming) and the Festival of the Hungry Ghosts. But Dongzhi is the only day on which families can, if they wish, register a newborn in the *kongsi* annals (the baby receives a *hongbao*, a cash gift in a red envelope for luck), or erect an ancestral tablet. Once consecrated into the *kongsi*, a "permanent residence" is set up and ancestral worship is secure. For families without male heirs — for only males can inherit the ancestral tablet and perpetuate the tradition — the clan house arrangement is a reassuring option.

When ancient customs ruled the day, married couples presented new shoes to their parents in conjunction with this festival. And the married daughter could look forward to a joyful reunion with her own family, Dongzhi being one of the few occasions when this was allowed. But her happiness was always short-lived, as she was not allowed to spend the night in her old home in the belief that it brought bad luck. (Married daughters became the property of their husbands' household and were discouraged from being too attached to their own.) Not surprisingly, this custom has fallen by the wayside in more recent times.

A feast rounds off the festivities of the day, bringing together gods, ancestors and man in the customary whirl of rituals and good cheer. The bond is strengthened and the cycle is complete. People may now embark on preparations to welcome the Chinese New Year, which begins with spring cleaning. But not before Dongzhi. This is one tradition that no one is inclined to break.

Rice Flour Balls in Sweet Syrup

In *sweet* versions of *tangyuan*, the rice flour balls are small and dainty. Bright colors are normally added, a combination of pink and white being the most popular. Some people prefer multi-colored pink, green and yellow balls. A recent trend is to combine *tangyuan* with canned fruit cocktail and serve it as a dessert in western style.

2 cups (250 g) glutinous rice flour, sifted
1 cup (250 ml) water
1 to 2 drops pink food coloring
1 can fruit cocktail (optional)

SYRUP
4 cups (1 liter) water
³/₄ cup (150 g) sugar
2 pandanus leaves (optional)
2 thin slices fresh ginger

Serves 4 to 6
Preparation time: 30 mins
Cooking time: 10 mins

1 Place the glutinous rice flour in a mixing bowl. Gradually pour in the water, mix well and then knead the dough until smooth. Divide the dough into 2 equal portions. Add the pink food coloring to 1 portion and knead until evenly colored. Leave the other portion white. On a flat surface, roll the dough into thin sausage-shaped cylinders, then break off small, even pieces from each cylinder. Roll each piece into a small ball between your palms. Place the rice flour balls on a large tray and cover with a cloth.

2 Bring a pot of water to a boil over high heat. In small batches, drop the rice flour balls into the boiling water, stirring gently to separate them, and simmer for 3 to 5 minutes until they float to the surface. Remove and immediately plunge the balls into a basin of iced water. Continue until all the rice flour balls are cooked. Drain the rice flour balls and set aside.

3 To make the Syrup, bring the water to a boil over medium heat in a saucepan. Add the sugar and stir until the sugar is dissolved. Add the pandanus leaves (if using) and ginger slices, and simmer for about 5 minutes. Finally add the cooked rice flour balls, mix well and remove from the heat.

4 Discard the pandanus leaves and ginger slices. Add the fruit cocktail (if using) to the *tangyuan*, spoon into individual serving bowls and serve hot or cold.

Rice Flour Balls in Soup Broth

In savory versions of *tangyuan*, the rice dough is rolled into tiny marble-sized balls and left uncolored. It is customary to serve this specialty for breakfast on the morning of the festival. The rice balls may be prepared and cooked well in advance.

2 cups (250 g) glutinous rice
   flour, sifted
1 cup (250 ml) water

BROTH
10 dried black Chinese mushrooms
6 oz (180 g) lean pork or 1 chicken
   breast, sliced into thin strips
2 tablespoons oil
4 shallots, finely sliced
1/2 cup (60 g) dried shrimp,
   rinsed and chopped with a
   cleaver
6 cups (1 1/2 liters) chicken stock
   or water combined with
   the soaking liquid from the
   mushrooms
3 spring onions, sliced to yield
   1 cup
3 to 4 lettuce leaves, minced to
   yield 1 cup

NOTE: The rice flour balls can be prepared a day in advance. Lay the rolled rice flour balls on a large tray, cover them with a damp cloth and set aside at room temperature until ready to be cooked.

1 Soak the Chinese mushrooms in hot water for about 30 minutes until soft, then drain and reserve the soaking liquid. Discard the stems and thinly slice the caps. Set aside.
2 Place the flour in a mixing bowl. Pour in the water, mix well and knead into a smooth dough. On a flat surface, roll the dough into narrow cylinders, then break off small, even pieces from each cylinder. Roll each piece into a marble-sized ball between your palms. Place the rice flour balls on a large tray, and cover them with a cloth.
3 Bring a pot of water to a boil over high heat. In small batches, drop the rice flour balls into the boiling water, stirring gently to separate them, and simmer for 3 to 5 minutes until they float to the surface. Remove and immediately plunge the balls into iced water. Continue until all the rice flour balls are cooked. Drain set aside.
4 To make the Broth, sear the pork or chicken strips over medium heat in a nonstick ungreased pan for 1 to 2 minutes. Remove and set aside. Heat the oil in a wok over high heat and stir-fry the shallot until fragrant and translucent, about 1 minute. Add the dried shrimp and stir-fry for 2 to 3 minutes until golden brown, then add the pork or chicken and mushroom slices. Pour in the stock and bring the ingredients to a boil, then simmer uncovered for 15 to 20 minutes. Finally add the cooked rice flour balls and remove from the heat.
5 Spoon the savory *tangyuan* into individual serving bowls. Serve hot, sprinkled with minced spring onion and lettuce leaves on top.

Serves 4 to 6   **Preparation time: 30 mins**   **Cooking time: 30 mins**

Chinese New Year

In the cycle of things, the end is followed by a new beginning, decay is followed by renewal. A new beginning — fresh, untouched and brimming with hope and endless possibilities — is a compelling reason for celebration.

The Chinese lunar calendar pinpoints the time of renewal, the beginning of a new cycle, at the onset of spring. This can be any day between the 20th of January and the 19th of February in the Gregorian calendar. This great event has been at different times called the Spring Festival (Chunjie), the Time of Beginning (Yuanchen), and the First Day (Yuanri). Mostly, it is known simply as Chinese New Year. Each new year signifies a turning point in the lives and fortunes of the Chinese. The slate is wiped clean; much is in store. It is everybody's wish to start off the new year well, a desire matched equally by the Chinese love of tradition, symbolism and ritual.

Preparations begin early, with spring cleaning commencing immediately after Dongzhi, the Winter Solstice. The momentum picks up in the following weeks, with people busy around the house painting, mending, sewing, cooking and shopping for food, clothes, gifts, ornaments and other items for the home. In keeping with the spirit of new beginnings, the house and its occupants must be, or at least should look, as fresh and as new as possible. For the same reason, everyone will try to fit an appointment with the hairdresser into their busy schedule for a cut, a perm or a completely new style. Such efforts will not go unnoticed, for it is the season of visitors and visiting.

The festive mood accelerates when the tradition of *songli* (presenting gifts) begins. Everybody is either giving or receiving. Seasonal delicacies that never go out of fashion — dried meats and sausages, ducks, prized delicacies such as shark's fin, abalone, fish maw and oysters, fruit, liquor and homemade cakes and pastries — are the most frequently exchanged.

Live poultry, however, no longer claims the sort of attention it used to, mainly because of the inconvenience attached to such a gift in modern times.

By New Year's Eve, the cupboard is filled to overflowing; it is considered unlucky to run out of supplies. The house is spick-and-span. Decorations, and more importantly, symbols of wealth, luck and happiness fill the home: potted *ju* (fruiting tangerine) trees, blooming peonies, narcissus, plum blossoms, pussy willows and chrysanthemums, paper scrolls bearing calligraphic characters representing wealth,

luck, prosperity and longevity, and drawings of the door gods, the god of wealth and cherubic children who carry enormous peaches or fish to affirm the auspicious theme. Some of these — such as *gan* (mandarin oranges, the embodiment of gold), *niangao* (sticky rice cakes representing growth and attainment of ambition) and the candy tray with its sweet contents conveying joy and happiness — are considered "weights," that add substance and solidity to the year. They remain on tables and altars throughout the season. This curious custom is called *chak nin* (a Cantonese expression meaning "weighting down the year"). For double insurance, circles of red paper are pasted on these "weapons." Or, if the objects are cylindrical, such as stems of sugar cane and large fruit, these will be trimmed with long strips of red paper.

The festivities commence with a family reunion dinner on New Year's Eve. Every member of the family is present for this grandest feast of the year, except for married daughters who will be with their in-laws. Once again, auspicious messages flow to the table — pork, chicken, duck, "treasures" from the sea such as oysters, abalone and sea moss — all are combined in winning formulas to attract wealth, luck and success, and are served in abundant quantities.

The feasting over, people busy themselves in the countdown to the great moment, putting the final touches or making last-minute preparations. Some might visit the night fairs in search of bargains. Men play mahjong. Children, dressed in new pajamas, are allowed to amuse themselves with fireworks, new toys or television until late into the night. The actual hour when the old gives way to the new is determined by the Chinese almanac, the Tongsheng and can be any time between midnight and two in the morning. (The Tongsheng is an

annual publication containing all sorts of invaluable information to the traditionalist, including the birthdays of gods, good and bad dates to get married, dates for planting crops, moving house or starting a business. It also gives predictions for the year.)

At home or in the neighborhood temple, people wait to worship and to seek blessings from the gods when the hour arrives. Each lunar year is dominated by an animal sign — a mouse, ox, tiger, hare, dragon, snake, horse, goat, monkey, rooster, dog or pig — twelve in all, which make up the major lunar calendar cycle. The beginning starts with a big bang, an explosion of fire-crackers, aimed at driving off evil spirits. The path is cleared. The year's designated animal enters. He dons the mantle of the ruler and begins his reign. The gods give their blessings and people exult in a renewed sense of hope.

Everyone emerges on the first day like butterflies out of their cocoons, in their new clothes, hair freshly combed and with bright happy faces. Everybody is on their best behavior. Tempers and tantrums are taboo. (The Chinese believe that the mood of the first day sets the rhythm for the rest of the year.) The younger generation pay respect to the older in accordance with the custom *bainian* where felicitations and wealth are extended to the elder in the celebrated salute: *gongxifacai* (*kung hei fatt choy* in Cantonese). In return, juniors receive a *yasuiqian* (lucky token), more commonly known as a *hongbao*. These are red paper packets stuffed with money. The amount varies; the relationship is what counts. Out of respect, nobody complains. It is the married people who give, while the children and the unmarried receive. This equation applies to *bainian*, the annual calls to pay respect or strengthen links in the name of tradition. In the workplace, employees can look forward to their own "red packets" when they return to work after the holidays. In view of the huge expenses the festival involves, many employers distribute "fat red packets" before the season begins and a "token of red" for luck when business reopens.

Cooking takes a back seat on the first day. Rather, people rely on the surplus from the day before, which is certain to be plentiful. Leftover meats can be salted or fried. More often than not, the leftovers from the reunion dinner are thrown into a pot and boiled for the après feast favorite, *chup kum* (*chop suey* to non-Chinese). Purists eat vegetarian food, deemed most appropriate for the first day.

On the second day, another appointment with luck and plenty takes place in the middle of the day when a feast is prepared to *hoi nin* (in Cantonese), meaning "to open the year." In Cantonese households, *hoi nin* is a splendid affair, almost (but not quite) as grand as the reunion dinner. Visits to pay respects to relatives and friends, when the young receive cash-filled red packets, can be observed on this day or any one of the first fifteen days of the New Year, except the third day, which is considered unlucky.

Day seven is Man's Day or Renri. The favored food is fish, especially the highly acclaimed *yusheng*, raw sliced fish tossed in a salad of sweet-sour pickles and crisps. For people who prefer cooked food, there is *yushengzhou*, a fish and rice gruel very popular with the Cantonese. Hakkas celebrate Renri with a soupy concoction of rice, tea, vegetables and dried shrimp known as *po lei char*. (The Hakkas are unique among the Chinese in having no province of their own. They are hence "guest people" as the word *hakka* suggests.) The Fukienese observe this day with a special brew containing seven health-promoting properties.

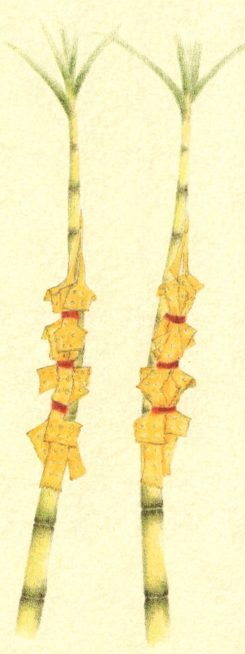

Day nine is the birthday of the Heavenly Emperor (Tiangong) alias the Jade Emperor. This mighty ruler of heaven is all set to receive tributes any time after midnight when the eighth day rolls into the ninth. The Fukienese convey this in a table resplendent with offerings framed with sugarcane plants, set up outside the front door to face the sky. Cane plants commemorate an event in their history when the Fukinese, fleeing persecution from a cruel Song Dynasty general, sought sanctuary in the sugarcane fields and were saved. The enemy had gone when they emerged from the fields. As it was the eve of the Jade Emperor's birthday, the people prepared a great feast and made offerings to the Jade Emperor for his timely intervention in a thanksgiving cere- mony that is today called *baitiangong*.

A visual feast of lanterns, fireworks, lion dances and — in some parts of China — a street parade of stilt dancers, costumed men with painted faces portraying legendary characters from Chinese folklore and literature, brings the festivities to a fitting climax on the fifteenth day. For yesterday's young swains, it was indeed the loveliest night of the year, the opportunity to view and meet, if lucky, a sweetheart or a bevy of dazzling prospects. Those were the days when young maidens were allowed out only one night a year, to be openly admired or appraised, all with a view to matrimony. The young ladies, chaperoned naturally, would be decked out in all their finery on this key night for that critical walk or ride down the promenade. Often no word was exchanged. A look was enough to send for the matchmaker. Despite the successes of such unions, post-war generations rejected the custom, preferring the modern, emancipated (but not less risky) approach in choosing and wooing.

Characteristically, as in all things Chinese, the fifteen day gala is riddled with superstitions. The belief is that if the New Year starts off badly, one will be dogged by bad luck for the rest of the year. To avoid this, a trial in itself, one has to refer to the baffling rules and regulations that time and generations have devised. First, debts must be settled before the last day of the old year as a debt is a stain on an otherwise clean slate. When feasting, one can enjoy, but should not get carried away and break things, since breaking a porcelain spoon, glass or any other object at the reunion table is a bad omen. Chipped crockery cannot be used for the occasion either, as imperfections ruin the unity of the reunion. To ensure "abundance all year long," the rice bin must be kept full throughout the festive season. On the first day, no one is allowed to sweep floors in case "luck will be swept away." Sharp objects should also be avoided on the first day because knives and scissors tend to "sever luck and ties." Black or dark blue, the funeral colors, should not be worn while observing the custom of *bainian*. Shades of red, pink, yellow and orange are desirable as no one can point a finger if things go badly for them. If people must gamble, they should not rush into it immediately after a bath as this is bad luck. The money- maker should not eat eel as this will be disastrous for business. Above all, people should not defile their own bright, clean beginning by swearing, uttering profanities or making morbid predictions.

As if treading the straight and narrow are not complicated enough, lurking evil spirits com-

pounds the scenario. They must be driven away since they have a way of spoiling man's enjoyment. Anything red works as this is the color demons most fear. They are also afraid of sudden noises. The crackling explosions of fire-crackers and the thunderous, reverberating sound of the lion dance are the most efficient means of deferring evil spirits while man revels uninterrupted.

Originally, the crackling explosions that made demons scurry for cover were *baozhu*, bamboo explosions, caused by the burning of bamboo stems. After gunpowder was invented during the Tang Dynasty, people rolled small amounts into paper cylinders with fuses attached to create the single explosive cracker. When the fuses are linked together, they form a chain, which when "fired" erupt in the repetitive, crackling explosions that are popularly identified with Chinese New Year. Traditionally, it was believed that a break in the chain of explosions was a bad omen.

Firecrackers are set off ceremoniously to introduce the "dancing lion," who is also the bearer of luck and good tidings. The "dance" involves a troupe of athletic youths maneuvering a monstrous, gaudily-painted paper mache skull mask attached to an equally gaudy cloth torso. To the accompaniment of clashing cymbals and thundering drums, the lion is sometimes teased and led through his antics by a big-headed deity, the *tatoufo*. (The lion has a fascination for this funny character waving his fan, and follows him wherever he goes.) In the hands of a skilled performer, the lion leaps, twists and rolls, flapping its ears and batting its eyelashes. In the course of a performance, it can be persuaded to "eat" oranges and peanuts, "chew" leaves of lettuce and even "drink" water, all for a *caiqing*, the reward gift. The

Accompanied by the crackling explosions of firecrackers and thunderous sounds of the drum, cymbal and gong, the lion dance was performed to ward off evil spirits in ancient China. It is now a symbol to usher in good luck, happiness and prosperity during festive occasions such as Chinese New Year, weddings and business openings.

most dramatic moment in the dance
is when the lion goes for the *caiqing*,
which is, fittingly, a *hongbao* (the
Chinese gift for all seasons) tied
together with a bunch of lettuce
and a sprig of ripe tangerines (*ju*).
The skill and courage of the lion is
undeniably tested in this maneuver
because the *caiqing* is always suspended from a high, hard-to-reach
place, such as the balcony or the
end of a bamboo pole anchored to
the second- or sometimes third-
storey window. But the lion always
gets the prize! He will appreciate a
round of exploding firecrackers in
place of applause, though he may jump
and stamp on the explosives as if in disdain
or anger. The dancing lion is a most engaging
character in spite of his fearsome appearance and
he never fails to captivate at any function to which
he is invited to perform the inaugural ceremonies.
It is at Chinese New Year, when the lovable
beast makes house calls in the manner of *bainian*,
that Chinese tradition is showcased at its best.

The year is considered well and truly begun
by day fifteen when the first moon turns on its full
face. Before long, people will resume their everyday
lives, the practical business of rebuilding life and
fortune, reinforced, it is imagined, with the auspicious elements they have so steadfastly surrounded
themselves with during the last few days of the old
year and the first two weeks of the new one.

Dried Sweet Barbecued Pork

These tasty dried pork sheets make an excellent Chinese New Year gift. Cut into finger-sized pieces and served with drinks or as hors d'oeuvres, they are popular with everyone. The sun-dried meat should be stored in the freezer between plastic sheets until they are ready to be barbecued, and are best when cooked over a charcoal fire. Cooked meat sheets keep well without refrigeration for 4 to 5 days and with refrigeration for 3 to 4 weeks. They should be brought to room temperature before eating or warmed in an oven or microwave.

4 lbs (2 kg) ground pork, preferably from the hind leg
$\frac{1}{2}$ cup (125 ml) soy sauce
$\frac{1}{2}$ cup (125 ml) oyster sauce
2 teaspoons fish sauce (*yue lo*)
2 $\frac{1}{2}$ cups (500 g) sugar
30 plastic bags (10 x 8 in/25 x 20 cm each)
Large trays, for drying

NOTE: A popular snack which goes very well with beer or wine, this delicious meat is also an excellent ingredient for making fried rice.

Makes 30 pieces
Preparation time: 30 mins + 7 hours drying
Cooking time: 5 to 10 mins per batch

1 Combine all the ingredients in a large mixing bowl and mix until well blended. Wet your hands and divide the mixture into 30 equal portions (each portion about $\frac{1}{3}$ cup). Roll each portion into a cylinder with your hands, then flatten slightly. Place each flattened cylinder in a plastic bag and use a rolling pin to roll it out into a thin layer, about $\frac{1}{8}$ in (3 mm) thick. Arrange the meat sheets in their plastic bags on large trays and dry in the sun for 6 to 7 hours, until the sheets are dry and firm. While they are drying, leave the mouth of the bags open and the top part of the bags lifted all the time to allow the moisture to escape. Turn the sheets over at 1 hour intervals, wiping away the moisture inside the bags with paper towels. If you can't dry the meat sheets in the sun, you may remove the sheets from the plastic and bake them on baking sheets in the oven using very low heat (140°F/60°C) for 4 to 5 hours, in several batches.

2 To serve, remove the dried meat sheets from the plastic bags and grill them in a pan or charcoal grill for 2 to 3 minutes on each side. Alternatively, sear the meat sheets in a heated nonstick pan for 2 to 3 minutes on each side. Cut the sheets into tiny squares or finger-sized slices and serve hot or at room temperature.

New Year's Cakes

The Chinese place great importance on anything that reflects their inner desires, and *niangao*, which means New Year's Cake, rhymes with "higher year," connoting the attainment of hopes and ambitions. In traditional households, *niangao* are left on tables, shelves or altars throughout the festive season as "weights," to secure solidity and substance in the ensuing year. They are also offered to the Kitchen God before he ascends to heaven to give his annual report on each household. This great event takes place on the 23rd or 24th day of the month preceding the Chinese New Year. The sweet, sticky cake is an incentive to obtain a sweetly-worded report from the god. Some households rely on the stickiness of the cake to moderate the Kitchen God's speech when recounting misdeeds. This sticky cake can be eaten by itself but is too bland for most palates and is often rolled in freshly grated coconut or cooked in batter. Sometimes it is sandwiched between pieces of taro or sweet potato and fried.

$2^3/_4$ cups (450 g) caster sugar

$^1/_2$ cup (125 ml) water

4 small round cake pans (each 4 in/10 cm in diameter)

2 large banana leaf sheets, soaked in hot water until soft

3 cups (360 g) glutinous rice flour, sifted

2 cups (500 ml) water

$1^1/_4$ cups (140 g) wheat starch (*tung meen fun*), sifted

$^1/_2$ cup (125 ml) oil

$^1/_2$ cup (125 ml) thin coconut milk

2 tablespoons Golden Syrup (page 110)

1 cup (100 g) freshly grated coconut, mixed with $^1/_2$ teaspoon salt (this serves 1 cake)

Makes 4 cakes
Preparation time: 1 hour + overnight setting
Cooking time: 4 hours

1 Bring the sugar and water to a boil in a saucepan, stirring until the sugar is dissolved. Reduce the heat to low, simmer for 15 to 20 minutes until the mixture has turned into a thick syrup. Remove and set aside to cool. Leave the syrup overnight.

2 Cut each banana leaf sheet into 16 strips each measuring 8 x $2^1/_2$ in (20 x 5 cm). Lay a strip across the center of a cake pan, with one end in the pan and the other end sticking up over one edge of the pan. Lay a second strip over the first, this time allowing the leaf to stick up on the other side. Lay third and fourth strips perpendicular to the first and second strips in the same manner, overlapping in the middle and sticking up on the sides. Repeat this process of laying the banana strips, until the base and sides of all 4 cake pans are lined. Trim off the extra lengths of banana leaf around the rims of the pans with a pair of scissors.

3 In a mixing bowl, mix the glutinous rice flour and water using a wooden spoon, or using a mixer at slow speed for 6 to 10 minutes. Stir in the wheat starch and oil, and thoroughly mix until well blended, then add the coconut milk, a little at a time, and stir well. Finally add the Golden Syrup and cooled syrup, mixing well after each addition, to produce a smooth batter.

4 Pour the batter equally into each cake pan. Place in a large heat-proof dish and steam in a covered wok or steamer over high heat for 3 to 4 hours, adding more hot water as needed. The cakes are done when they have turned brown. Carefully remove the rice cakes from the steamer and pour off any liquid on the surface of the cakes. Allow to cool and set at room temperature overnight.

5 To remove the rice cakes from the pans, run a knife between the leaves and the sides to loosen, then place a plate over the pan and

invert it. Refrigerate the rice cakes in their banana leaf coverings until ready to use.

6 When ready to eat, peel off the banana leaf coverings and cut each cake into quarters, then slice into thick pieces. Place in a heatproof dish and steam in a wok or steamer for 5 to 10 minutes until soft. Remove from the heat. While the cake is still hot, dab each piece in the grated coconut, turning over a few times, until it is well coated on all sides. Arrange the coated pieces on a platter and serve immediately.

NOTES: If banana leaves are not available, use aluminum foil to line the cake pans or just grease them, then steam and store the rice cakes in them until ready to eat. To serve the rice cake deep-fried in batter, prepare a batter by combining $1\frac{1}{2}$ cups (160 g) of long grain rice flour, $\frac{3}{4}$ cup (185 ml) of water, 6 tablespoons of coconut milk and a pinch of salt to make a smooth batter. This yields enough batter to deep-fry 1 rice cake. Slice the rice cake into $\frac{1}{2}$-in (1-cm) thick slabs. Dip the pieces in the batter to coat them evenly and deep-fry in very hot oil over medium heat for about 2 minutes on each side. Serve hot or at room temperature.

Festive Arrowhead Stir-fry

The arrowhead bulb or *see koo* (in Cantonese) is a delicious bulb appearing in early spring. It is widely associated with Chinese New Year. It has a taste that is a cross between a potato and a water chestnut. The Chinese prepare arrowhead bulbs in soups or cook them by themselves, sliced into disks. Another favorite method is to partner them with one of the dried or smoked meats of the season. Potted *see koo* (shown at left) make charming houseplants for the Chinese New Year. To the Chinese, the plant is symbolic as well as decorative, connoting progeny and all its values.

7 oz (200 g) **Yunnan** or **Parma ham** or **back bacon**

1 ¹/₂ tablespoons oil

1 clove garlic, minced

8 to 10 arrowhead bulbs (*see koo*), shoots discarded, peeled and cut into large wedges

2 tablespoons soy sauce

1 tablespoon oyster sauce

¹/₂ teaspoon sugar

Serves 4 to 6
Preparation time: 15 mins
Cooking time: 20 mins

1 Soak the ham in boiling water for 20 minutes, then drain and slice thinly. Set aside.

2 Heat the oil in a wok over high heat. Stir-fry the garlic until fragrant and golden brown, about 30 seconds. Add the bulb wedges, ham or bacon and stir-fry for 2 to 3 minutes, seasoning with the soy sauce and oyster sauce. Add enough water to just cover the ingredients, then bring to a boil. Reduce the heat to medium, cover and simmer for about 15 minutes or until the sauce has reduced to half. Season with the sugar and remove from the heat.

3 Transfer to a serving platter and serve immediately.

NOTES: If you cannot find arrowhead bulbs, you can replace them with 14 oz (400 g) potatoes or taro, peeled and cut into wedges, then prepared as instructed in the recipe. Chinese Yunnan ham is salted pork belly strips that have been cured with sugar and thick soy sauce, and then air dried. They are sold in butcher shops and Chinese groceries, and widely available during Chinese New Year, along with smoked ducks and Chinese sausages. Parma ham or back bacon may be used instead.

Yusheng Sashimi Salad

This delectable dish tops the menu at every Chinese restaurant in Southeast Asia during the 2-week Chinese New Year period. It is considered an auspicious dish as the term used for mixing the salad together sounds almost the same in Cantonese as the words for good luck and prosperity.

SALAD
1 medium carrot
1 medium daikon radish
1 taro (about 1 lb/500 g)
$\frac{1}{2}$ teaspoon each red and green food coloring (optional)
$\frac{1}{2}$ cup (60 g) sliced preserved sweet papaya or melon (see note)
$\frac{1}{2}$ cup (60 g) sliced sweet pickled ginger (see page 38)
$\frac{1}{2}$ cup (150 g) pomelo or grapefruit pulp, peeled and shredded
$\frac{1}{2}$ cup (50 g) prepared jellyfish (see note), sliced (optional)

SAUCE
2 teaspoons sesame oil
5 tablespoons Chinese plum sauce
3 tablespoons lime juice

FISH SASHIMI AND SEASONINGS
5 oz (150 g) fresh salmon fillets
1 tablespoon Crispy Garlic (see page 28)
2 tablespoons sliced fresh ginger
$\frac{1}{2}$ teaspoon ground white pepper
1 tablespoon lime juice

GARNISHES
4 tablespoons crushed roasted unsalted peanuts
$\frac{1}{2}$ tablespoon five spice powder
1 tablespoon roasted sesame seeds
Sprigs of coriander leaves
2 packets fried noodles or *yusheng* crisps or 10 wonton wrappers, deep-fried until crispy, crushed

1 Prepare the Salad first by grating the carrot, radish and taro into long, thin strands using a mandoline or spiral slicer if available, then squeeze them dry. Place the carrot and radish in separate mounds on a large serving platter. Mix half of the taro strands with red food coloring and the other half with green food coloring (if using), and leave to stand for 20 minutes. Deep-fry the red and green taro strands separately over medium heat until crispy, 3 to 5 minutes. Remove and drain on paper towels, then place them in separate mounds on the platter with the carrot and radish. Prepare the rest of the Salad ingredients and arrange in separate mounds on the same platter.
2 Combine the Sauce ingredients in a serving bowl and mix well.
3 To serve, place everything on the dining table: the platter of Salad, the bowl of Sauce, a plate with the raw fish, small bowls with the fish Seasonings next to it and a plate with the Garnishes. Start with the Fish Sashimi and Seasonings — toss the raw fish in the Seasonings and place it on the platter with the Salad. Pour the Sauce over all the ingredients and sprinkle the Garnishes on top. Then, invite your guests to toss the salad together with chopsticks while standing around the table repeating the words *"lo hei, lo hei, …"* to ensure good luck.

NOTES: Preserved sweet papaya or melon are candied slices of the fruits that are coated with sugar. They are sold in Chinese grocery stores. Pomelo is a citrus fruit that is larger than grapefruit but not as juicy. Prepared jellyfish are sold in ready-to-eat packets.

Serves 4 to 6   Preparation time: 1 hour

Traditional Chinese Jiaozi

These traditional dumplings, *jiaozi*, are a favorite in northern China. The entire family is involved in the preparation which is then served at the reunion dinner on New Year's Eve.

10 oz (300 g) ground pork
7 oz (200 g) Chinese chives or
  Chinese cabbage, minced and
  squeezed dry
1 teaspoon grated ginger
3 spring onions, minced
40 wonton or dumpling wrappers
Soy sauce or oyster sauce, for
  dipping

MARINADE
1 tablespoon soy sauce
1 teaspoon salt
1 teaspoon sesame oil
1 teaspoon rice wine or dry sherry
1 teaspoon freshly ground black
  pepper
$\frac{1}{2}$ teaspoon ground white pepper

Makes 40 dumplings
Preparation time: 1 hour + 30 mins
  to marinate
Cooking time: 30 mins

1 Combine the Marinade ingredients in a small bowl and mix well. Pour the Marinade over the ground pork and mix in one direction until well combined. Cover with a cloth and allow to marinate for at least 30 minutes in the refrigerator, then add all the minced vegetables to the marinated ground pork and mix well.

2 To make the dumplings, place 1 tablespoon of the Filling onto the center of a wrapper and dab the edges with a little water. Fold the wrapper in half to form a semicircle, enclosing the filling, and press the edges together to stick. If using a square wrapper, fold in half diagonally to form a triangle. Repeat until all the filling is used up.

3 Bring a large pot of water to a boil over high heat. Carefully drop 10 to 15 dumplings into the boiling water and gently stir so that they do not stick together, then cover and return to a boil. Add 1 cup of cold water to the pot, cover and bring the dumplings to a boil again. Repeat to bring the dumplings to a boil for the third time, then when all the dumplings float to the surface, remove them from the pot. Transfer the dumplings to a serving platter greased with a little sesame oil to prevent them from sticking together. Continue to cook the remaining dumplings in the same manner.

4 Serve the dumplings immediately with dipping bowls of soy sauce or oyster sauce on the side.

NOTES: The same recipe is also used to make pot stickers (*guotie*). The difference is that instead of boiling, the dumplings are pan-fried in a skillet by 1 tablespoons of oil over medium heat for 3 minutes until browned on the bottom and cooked through. To ensure the dumplings are well cooked, cover the skillet for part of the time while frying them.

Vital Ingredients

Alkaline water (*kan sui* in Cantonese), also known as lye water, is a dilute alkaline solution (made from sodium or potassium carbonate) added in small amounts to noodles, rice dumplings or cakes to add color and texture to the starch. Small bottles of alkaline water are sold in Chinese grocery shops. If you cannot find it, replace with the same amount of baking soda solution (made from 1 part of baking soda dissolved in 1 part of water).

Arrowhead bulbs (*see koo* in Cantonese) are crisp, white-fleshed bulbs similar in shape to water chestnuts, but larger. They have a starchy white flesh inside and are often added to braised meat or vegetable dishes, and are also good when stir-fried. Arrowhead bulbs are widely cultivated in China and Japan, and exported to countries with large Chinese communities during the lunar New Year period. Look for bulbs with short shoots in the Chinese markets, as these are younger and sweeter. Cut off the shoot and peel the skin, then cook them whole or sliced. Potatoes or taro may be used as a substitute.

Bamboo leaves are sold dried in bundles. They are long and narrow, normally measuring about 15 to 18 in (38 to 45 cm) long, and are used to wrap rice dumplings (see page 85). Soak them in water overnight before using. Store the dried leaves in a cool, dry place and they will keep for up to a year.

Bamboo shoots are the young sprouts of the bamboo plant. Fresh cream-colored shoots can be purchased in Asian markets — remove the green outer leaves and boil the tender shoot inside for 1 hour. Canned, frozen and vacuum-packed bamboo shoots are widely available now and are more convenient since they are precooked. Rinse them well before using (and if using canned shoots it's a good idea to "freshen" them up by boiling for several minutes). Unused portions may be stored in the refrigerator for up to a week covered with cold water if the water is changed daily.

Banana leaves are widely used to wrap foods before steaming or grilling them, and they impart a wonderful fragrance to many dishes. Packets of folded fresh or frozen banana leaves are available in well-stocked supermarkets and Asian markets. If you cannot find them, use aluminum foil sheets instead. Before using, the leaves need to be softened either by placing them in a tub and pouring boiling water over them or briefly heating them over a low flame.

Bangkuang is a large, globe-shaped tuber, tapering slightly to one end like a top, with a papery beige skin enclosing a crisp, white flesh. It is known in Latin America as jicama and is often confusingly referred to as a "turnip" in Malaysia and Singapore. Slightly sweet and juicy when small and young, it tends to become fibrous with age.

Bangkuang can be eaten raw (usually with a dip) or cooked with spices. Its sweet and crunchy flesh is a popular ingredient in salads.

Black Chinese mushrooms, also known as shiitake mushrooms, are normally sold dried. There are many different varieties and grades, with colors ranging from light brown to almost black, often with speckles. The best grades are plump and heavy. Top grade dried mushrooms are expensive, but worth it for their smooth succulence when braised or steamed in a rich sauce. When using dried mushrooms, soak them in hot water for 20 to 30 minutes to soften them, then drain. Remove and discard the stems.

Black sea moss is a fine, hair-like dried seaweed, valued in Chinese cooking because its Cantonese name *fatt choy* rhymes with the words for "prosperity." When soaked in water, the sea moss becomes soft and smooth. It has little taste on its own but takes on the flavors of foods it is combined with. Black sea moss may be purchased from Chinese grocery stores or herbal shops in small plastic packages. Soak it in water for about 15 minutes until soft, then rinse in a couple of changes of water before using.

Bok choy (also known as Chinese chard) is a crunchy, leafy green vegetable used widely in Chinese stir-fries. Baby bok choy is the smaller version, with plump white stalks and dark green leaves. Fresh bok choy is available year-round in most supermarkets and Asian markets. Look for thick, firm stalks and unblemished green leaves. Swiss chard makes a good substitute.

Chicken stock is an important ingredient in many Chinese stir-fry dishes, soups and sauces. Most cooks now prefer to use canned chicken stock, bouillon cubes or stock powder. You can easily make your own chicken stock at home by bringing 1 lb (500 g) chicken bones or one 7-oz (200-g) chicken breast, 10 cups (2 $\frac{1}{2}$ liters) water, 2 stalks of celery, 4 bunches of coriander leaves (cilantro), 2 slices ginger and 8 white peppercorns to a boil in a stockpot. Simmer covered over low heat for 1 to 1 $\frac{1}{2}$ hours, skimming off the foam and fat that float to the surface, until the stock reduces to half. Season with salt and remove from the heat, then strain. This yields 5 cups (1 $\frac{1}{4}$ liters) of stock.

Chilies have become an essential ingredient in Chinese cooking and several different varieties are used. **Finger-length red chilies** are the most common, and are moderately hot. **Dried red chilies** of this variety are stir-fried whole or

ground to make chili flakes. Tiny **bird's-eye chilies** are much hotter, and are also available dried. To reduce the heat of the chilies while retaining the flavor, remove the seeds before slicing or mincing the casings.

Chinese cabbage is prized for its mild, sweet taste. Also known as napa cabbage, it has crinkly, pale green leaves on long and wide, ribbed stalks. It is pleasantly crisp when raw and has a slightly sweet flavor which intensifies after long, slow cooking. This vegetable grows in two forms: long and slender, and short and round. There is no difference in the flavor; both varieties may be used for the recipes in this book. Chinese cabbage is available year round. Choose firm, tightly packed heads with fresh leaves.

Chinese celery is a small, pungent plant, with leaves resembling Italian parsley (which makes a good substitute) or oversized coriander leaves (cilantro). It is mainly used as a flavoring herb rather than a vegetable. The leaves are often used to garnish soups and noodle dishes. Whole Chinese celery stems with roots can be refrigerated for up to a week by placing the

roots in a jar containing a little water or wrapping them with a moist paper towel and then putting them inside a plastic bag.

Chinese chives or **garlic chives** look very similar to spring onions, with long green and slightly flat leaves that resemble coarse blades of grass. They have a distinct garlicky flavor and are far more pungent than Western chives. Sold in bunches in Asian markets and well-stocked supermarkets; spring onions or normal chives may be substituted.

Cloud ear fungus, also known as black fungus, comes in gray to black curly sheets that are normally sold dried packed in small plastic bags in Chinese grocery stores. They look like delicate, paper-thin leaves and crumble easily. They must be rinsed and soaked in water before using, and will then expand into translucent sheets two to three times their original size. Remove the hard knobs and rinse well after soaking, as dirt is often lodged in the folds. Once cooked, they are almost flavorless, but the texture is silky and slightly crunchy. Though closely related, **wood ear fungus** is bigger and has a cruder and thicker texture, however it can be

used as a substitute. If neither one is available, omit from the recipe.

Coconut cream or **milk** is mainly used in desserts in Chinese cooking. While freshly pressed coconut milk has more flavor, coconut cream and milk are widely available in cans and carton packets that are quick and convenient to use. Consistencies vary from brand to brand, so use your judgment and dilute with water as needed. Thick coconut milk is obtained from coconut cream by diluting by half with water; and thin coconut milk is half again as diluted as thick milk. If you prefer to make your own from fresh coconuts, you first need to open the coconut by tapping firmly on the center with the blunt end of a cleaver until a crack appears. Drain the juice and continue tapping until the coconut cracks into two. Place the coconut halves in a moderate oven for 15 to 20 minutes until the flesh shrinks away from the shell. Remove the flesh and use a vegetable peeler to shave off the brown outer skin, then grate it in a blender or food processor (this will yield about 4 cups of grated flesh). For fresh coconut cream, add $1/2$ cup water to the grated flesh of 1 coconut, knead it a few times, then strain it with your fist or using a muslin cloth or cheesecloth. This should yield about $1/2$ cup of coconut cream. Thick coconut milk is obtained by adding 1 cup of water to the grated coconut flesh, which will yield about 1 cup of thick coconut milk. Thin coconut milk is obtained by adding another cup of water to the already pressed coconut flesh and squeezing it a second time; this will yield 1 cup of thin coconut milk. As mentioned above,

you may also obtain thin coconut milk by diluting thick coconut milk or coconut cream with water.

Coriander leaves (cilantro) are a ubiquitous herb in Chinese cooking and are often referred to as Chinese parsley. These delicate green leaves have a fresh aroma and flavor and are used almost exclusively as a garnish in Chinese cooking. Fresh coriander leaves will keep for 5 to 6 days in the refrigerator if you wash and dry them thoroughly before placing them in a plastic bag. Italian parsley or basil may be used as a substitute, although the flavor is not the same.

Daikon radish, also called white radish or Chinese radish (and known in many Southeast Asian countries as *lobak*), is a vegetable that looks like an oversized white carrot. A popular pickle ingredient in Japanese cooking, Chinese cooks use this vegetable more in soups. Smaller radishes have a milder flavor and finer texture than larger ones. Chinese radishes are usually peeled and sliced before cooking. They have a very thin skin that can be scraped off easily with a knife or vegetable peeler.

Dried bean curd skin is a thin, cream-colored sheet made from soybean milk solids. It comes in flat sheets and is sold in plastic packets in the dry-goods sections of Chinese food shops. Dried bean curd skin packed in plastic bags will keep for up to a year when stored in a cool, dry place.

Dried Chinese sausages (*lap cheong*) are sweet and aromatic finger-sized pork sausages seen hanging

in bunches in Chinese shops or in netting bags. They are bright red in color, rather hard and chewy, and are never eaten raw or by themselves, but are sliced and stir-fried or braised with other ingredients. They must be cooked before eating. Chinese sausages keep well in a dry place and can be stored refrigerated for several months. Briefly soak them in water and remove the outer skin before slicing. Dried sweet salami or hard, sweet jerky may be used as a substitute.

Dried cuttlefish is sold in plastic packets in many different forms — shredded and flavored (to be eaten as a snack), or plain in flat sheets (to be used as an ingredient in cooking). It has a strong flavor and is used in soups and other dishes. Purchase unflavored dried cuttlefish (either in sheets or shreds) for the recipes in this book. Before using, soak the cuttlefish in water for several hours to soften it. Dried squid is a good substitute.

Dried oysters are shucked and sun-dried, and may be gold to reddish or dark brown in color. They come in various sizes. A popular ingredient in Chinese cooking because of their rich flavor, dried oysters are sold in plastic packets in Asian food stores or supermarkets. Dried oysters must be rinsed and then soaked in cold water for at least 1 hour before using. Always reserve the soaking liquid, as it is very flavorful and can be added to other dishes. But do not use the last part of the soaking liquid as it contains the grit released when the oysters are soaked. Dried oysters may be stored in an airtight jar indefinitely.

Dried shrimp are tiny saltwater shrimp which have been dried in the sun. They come in different sizes and the really small ones have their heads and shells intact. Look for bright orange-pink and plump dried shrimp; avoid those with a grayish appearance or an unpleasant smell. Dried shrimp are sold in all Asian shops and will keep for several months when stored in a dry place. Soak the dried shrimp in water to soften before using.

Fish sauce is the amber-colored liquid made from salted, fermented fish or shrimp. It has a very pungent, salty flavor in its pure form. It is widely used throughout Asia and many countries manufacture their own variety. You will find fish sauce from Thailand, Vietnam, the Philippines and China in Asian markets. Always look for a quality brand for a better flavor. Refrigerate after opening.

Five spice powder is a ground spice mixture consisting of star anise, fennel, cloves, cinnamon and pepper. It is an essential ingredient in Chinese cooking and is normally used in stews, braised dishes and marinades. Five spice powder is sold in small plastic packets or jars in Chinese grocery stores or the spice section of supermarkets.

Gingko nuts are oval and cream-colored, with hard shells that must be cracked open with a nutcracker. The inner meats have a nutty, slightly bitter flavor and must be soaked in boiling water to loosen their skins. Gingko nuts are known for their medicinal properties and often used in Chinese herbal prepa-

rations. Shelled nuts may be purchased frozen or refrigerated in vacuum-sealed packs in Chinese grocery stores. Canned gingko nuts are also available but have far less flavor — when using them, add them at the final stages of cooking.

Glass noodles or **bean thread noodles** (also called cellophane noodles, *tang hoon* or *fensi*) are fine, transparent noodles made from ground mung beans. They are sold in small bundles in plastic packets in Chinese grocery shops and are difficult to cut or separate before soaking. For this reason, buy them in the amounts needed for each recipe. Before cooking, place the required amount in a bowl and add enough warm water to cover the noodles. They will soften after 10 minutes of soaking. Once cooked, glass noodles become almost transparent. They are bland and take on the flavor of the seasonings they are prepared with.

Glutinous rice or **sticky rice** is a variety of short grain rice that is more starchy than normal rice when cooked, so the grains stick together instead of separating the way long grain rice does. Widely used in desserts throughout Asia, it is eaten as a staple in countries like Thailand. Two types of glutinous rice are available, white and black, but only the white variety is generally used in Chinese cooking. Glutinous rice needs to be soaked in water overnight or for at least 3 hours before cooking as otherwise it does not fully cook through and remains hard in the center.

Hoisin sauce is a sweet brown

sauce made from yellow soybeans, sugar, vinegar, sesame oil and spices such as cinnamon and star anise. It is added to sauces and marinades, and is a favorite condiment on its own for barbecued meats and spring rolls. Hoisin sauce is sold in cans, jars and bottles.

Hot bean sauce or **chili bean sauce** is a smooth red sauce made from yellow bean sauce mixed with chilies. This very spicy sauce is an essential ingredient in many Sichuan and Korean dishes. It is sold in cans and jars in most supermarkets and Chinese grocery stores.

Kailan, also known as Chinese kale or Chinese broccoli, is a crunchy green vegetable with slender, dark green stalks, dark green

leaves and white flowers. The entire vegetable may be boiled, steamed or stir-fried. Choose kailan with unwilted, dark green leaves and narrow stalks and discard the tough thick ends of the stalks. Refrigerate, unwashed in a plastic bag for no more than 2 to 3 days.

Lily buds, also known as golden needles or lily flowers, are the unopened flowers of a type of lily. They appear like long golden ribbons and add an earthy flavor and texture to stir-fries and soups. An important ingredient in Chinese vegetarian dishes, lily buds are normally sold dried in plastic bags in Chinese apothecaries or grocery stores. Choose lighter, honey-colored strands, as darker brown lily buds are old. Before using, briefly soak the lily buds in water and remove the hard stem. Store in an airtight jar in a cool, dry place.

Lotus leaves are the dried leaves of the lotus plant, often used in Chinese cooking to wrap dishes before steaming them. They impart a distinctive, sweet aroma to foods which they are used to wrap. Though fresh lotus leaves can also be used, dried lotus leaves are more readily available and are sold in packets in most Chinese grocery shops. Soak the dried leaves in hot water for at least 20 minutes before using them to wrap foods.

Lotus seeds are the large yellow seeds of the sacred lotus plant. Both fresh and dried seeds are available; either whole or halved with the bitter central core (endosperm) removed. They are also sold precooked in cans or vacuum-sealed packs, and dried seeds are available in plastic bags in Chinese grocery and herbal shops. **Dried lotus seeds** need to be soaked for several hours before cooking. Lotus seeds are popular in soups and desserts, and are ground up with sugar to make a sweet paste filling for buns, mooncakes and pancakes. Readymade sweet lotus seed paste is sold in cans and plastic packets also, and there is a special type used for mooncakes which is labeled as such.

Magnolia petals are sold dried in packets in Chinese herbalist shops. These pale yellow, dried petals of the Chinese magnolia flower are commonly used in Chinese herbal preparations to make tonics or soups. They are believed to ease nasal congestion. Soak them in water for 30 minutes before using.

Maltose syrup is a type of syrup made from malted grains which is used in Chinese cooking to coat barbecued meats. It can be purchased in bottles in supermarkets. Honey or golden syrup may be used as a substitute.

Mung bean flour is a fine powder ground from roasted green mung beans. Commonly used in Asian cooking, it adds texture to rice cakes and noodles. It can be purchased from Asian markets in small paper packets that come in various colors.

Oyster sauce is a thick brown Chinese seasoning sauce made from a mixture of dried oyster extract, soy sauce, sugar and salt. A popular sauce sold in bottles in most supermarkets, it intensifies the flavor of foods. It is often drizzled over cooked vegetables, added to stir-fries, sauces and marinades, or served as a dipping sauce on its own. Choose a brand low in salt and free of **MSG** if you can find one. A vegetarian version prepared from mushroom extract is available and is an excellent substitute as real oyster sauce can contain harmful chemicals.

Pandanus leaves are the long and slender, blade-like green leaves of the pandanus palm, a member of the screwpine family. The leaves impart a fresh floral fragrance and are used as an air freshener across Asia as well as to perfume desserts and rice dishes. Their intense green color is also used as a natural food coloring. Look for fresh leaves in Asian markets. If unavailable, substitute bottled pandanus essence or rose or vanilla essence.

Plum sauce is a thick, honey-colored sweet and sour sauce made from Chinese plums stewed with sugar, salt, ginger and a touch of chili. It makes a popular dip for meats or spring rolls and is available in cans or jars in most supermarkets.

Preserved bean curd, also known as fermented bean curd, has the consistency and pungency of strong smelling cheese. It comes in two main varieties: either red (colored with red rice), or brown, and chili and rice wine are often added. **Red preserved bean curd** (*nam yee*) has chili and hoisin sauce added to it during fermentation. Both red and brown varieties are sold in cans and jars in Chinese grocery shops. Once opened, it must be refrigerated but will keep almost indefinitely.

Red dates, also known as Chinese jujubes, are sold in small plastic bags in supermarkets and Chinese herbalist shops. They have a crinkly, red skin and are about the size of olives. Unlike Western dates, these dried dates have a fruity fragrance similar to raisins. They are never eaten by themselves, but are added to soups and stews as a flavoring. Red dates are often used in herbal preparations, as they are believed to improve blood circulation.

Rice flour is ground from rice grains and two very different varieties are used in Chinese cooking — normal rice flour, which is ground from regular long grain rice, and **glutinous rice flour**. Both are sold in plastic packets but be careful not to confuse the two as the results will be very different depending on which type is used.

Rice noodles are made from rice flour but there are various types and they have different flavors and uses. Flat, broad rice noodles are known as **rice sticks** or *hor fun* (*kway teow* in Hokkien) whereas very thin, fine rice noodles are known as **rice vermicelli** or **rice threads** (*beehoon* or *mifen*). In Asia, both fresh and dried rice noodles are commonly available however outside of Asia only the dried packet varieties are generally found. Fresh rice noodles should be blanched in hot water for 1 minute to remove the oil that is added to keep the strands from sticking together, then drained and used as directed in the recipe. **Dried rice vermicelli** should be soaked in water to soften before using. **Dried rice sticks** or **round rice noodles** need to be boiled for 5 to 7 minutes, depending on the thickness.

Rice wine has a relatively low alcohol content and is fermented from freshly steamed glutinous rice. Rice wine is available in bottles in most Chinese grocery shops or liquor stores. For Chinese cooking, buy the best grade of Shao Xing rice wine. If unavailable, use pale dry sherry or sake instead. Store at room temperature.

Sago beads are tiny dried beads made from the starch of the sago palm. They soften and turn transparent when cooked, and have a gluey texture but very little flavor of their own as they mainly consist of starch. Sago beads are widely used in desserts in Asian cooking, generally combined with sugar and coconut cream. Dried sago beads are available in packets in the dry

goods section of Asian food stores. Tapioca pearls may be used as a substitute.

Sesame oil is extracted from roasted (darker brown oil) or raw (lighter colored oil) sesame seeds. Chinese sesame oil is a rich, amber color, unlike the paler unroasted Middle Eastern sesame oils. It is used mainly as a seasoning in sauces and marinades, and as a finish to many dishes, but never as a base oil for stir-frying, as high heat turns it bitter. Buy it in small bottles as it loses its aroma quickly once opened.

Shark's fins are prized for their texture and nutritional properties rather than for their flavor. True shark's fin is very expensive and increasingly controversial these days due to the ecologically cruel way in which the fins are harvested without first killing the sharks. Preparing a dried fin takes several days, so ready-prepared versions are much easier as you just need to soak and then cook them. The fins you buy in most stores have already been processed and look like thin glass noodles, and bean thread or glass noodles actually make a very good substitute. Vegetarian shark's fins made from mung beans can be purchased in Chinese vegetarian food stores. These can be used to replace real shark's fins in shark's fin soup and most people cannot tell the difference since the real fins are flavorless.

Soy sauce is a universal bottled ingredient in all Chinese kitchens and is naturally brewed from soybeans, wheat or barley flour, sugar, salt and water. There are many

varieties — the two most common for cooking being light and black soy sauce. Regular soy sauce (also known as light soy sauce) is saltier and thinner and is used in Chinese cooking as a seasoning and as a table dip. **Black soy sauce** is darker, thicker and richer in color, and slightly sweeter in taste. Used as a browning agent for roasting or braising meats, it contributes color as well as flavor. Also available are mushroom-flavored soy sauces, seasoned soy sauces for seafood and chili soy sauces. Store soy sauce at room temperature.

Star anise is a star-shaped dried seed pod with eight points, each of which contains a flat seed. It has a licorice flavor and aroma similar to fennel seed or aniseed. It is usually added whole to dishes and the pods are removed before the dish is served.

Tapioca flour or **tapioca starch** is also known as cassava flour. This starch from the cassava root is used as a thickening agent, like cornflour or cornstarch. Combined with rice flour, it adds a translucent sheen and springiness to cakes and pastries. Packets of tapioca flour are available in Asian food stores. Cornstarch

may be used as a substitute although it has a slightly softer texture.

Sweet Chinese pickles are commonly made at home by soaking finely-sliced vegetables like carrots, cauliflower florets, *daikon* radish, cabbage, garlic, ginger, shallots or spring onion bulbs in sweetened rice vinegar. Prepared pickles are sold in packets, jars or cans in Chinese grocery shops. The recipe for making your own pickles is on page 38.

Taro is a starchy root vegetable that is often prepared like a potato. It has a brown and hairy outer skin that must be removed before cooking. Its flesh may be pinkish, purple, beige or white, with the texture of a potato but a unique taste and flavor. It is normally boiled, baked, fried or steamed. There are two kinds of taro — a larger one and a miniature taro similar in size to a baby potato. Choose taros that are dry and firm. They may be stored in a cool and dry place for up to a week. In Asia, taro is often mistakenly referred to as "yam" — although it is not related to yams or sweet potatoes, which are quite different in flavor and texture. The closest substitute is potato.

Water chestnuts are grown in muddy ponds; the chestnuts are about the size of a small plum, with a dark brown skin, and are often sold with some dried mud still clinging to them. A gourmet's delight because of their crunchy and juicy-sweet white flesh, water chestnuts are available fresh, processed and canned, and are found in most supermarkets in some form. Fresh water chestnuts need to

be peeled before using. Rinse them well to remove any dirt, and soak them in water after peeling to avoid discoloration. Water chesnuts can be stored up to a week in the refrigerator covered in water inside a container if the water is changed daily. Canned water chestnuts are not nearly as tasty as fresh ones.

Water chestnut flour, also known as water chestnut powder, is a starchy flour made from ground dried water chestnuts. It is used in much the same way as cornstarch — as a thickener and coating agent — and like cornstarch should be mixed with a small amount of water to create a solution before being added to sauces. Small boxes of this flour are obtainable from Asian food stores. Cornstarch is a good substitute.

Wheat noodles are made from wheat flour, salt and water, sometimes with eggs added. Chinese wheat noodles are white or yellow, and are available fresh or dried. They come in varying shapes and widths ranging from round and very thin to large and somewhat square. Thinner varieties are used in light soups, while the thicker ones work well in heavier soups and stir-fries. Wheat noodles are often called "egg noodles" even though most do not contain any egg and get their yellow color from food dye instead. The thinnest wonton or Hong Kong noodles can be bought fresh or dried, but thicker yellow noodles (Hokkien *mee*), as thick as a slim chopstick, are only sold fresh. Deep-fried *yee fu* Cantonese noodles are only available dried. Fresh noodles should be shaken and blanched in boiling water for up to 1 minute, then rinsed in cold water and drained. Dried noodles should be boiled until soft without any pre-soaking, then rinsed in cold water and drained. The boiling time for dried wheat noodles depends on the thickness, but is generally 5 to 7 minutes.

Wheat starch (*tung meen fun* in Cantonese) is a white, starchy flour milled from gluten-free wheat. It is an essential ingredient in making Chinese *dianxin* (or *dim sum* in Cantonese) and desserts — it is combined with tapioca flour to make the transparent wrapping for popular dumplings such as *xiajiao* (shrimp dumplings). Packets of Chinese brand wheat starch flour can be purchased from Chinese grocery stores.

Winter melons or **winter gourds** (*donggua*) are a very large variety of gourd or squash that looks like a round watermelon. The skin is green, often with a white waxy covering, and the flesh is pale green with small, white seeds. Winter melon has a very mild flavor and when cooked it absorbs the flavors of whatever it is cooked with. It also becomes beautifully translucent when cooked and has a very smooth texture. You can buy winter melons whole or already cut into pieces in Asian markets. It should be used immediately, as it tends to dry out quickly.

Wonton wrappers or **wonton skins** are square or round uncooked wrappers made of flour, eggs and water. Available in different sizes and thicknesses, they are cooked with a wide variety of fillings. The thin ones work best in soups, while the thicker ones are best for frying. Wonton wrappers are available frozen or fresh. Look for stacks of them wrapped in plastic in the refrigerator or freezer section. Store them chilled but thaw to room temperature before using.

Yellow bean paste (*tau cheo* in Hokkien) is also known as fermented bean paste or black bean paste and is similar to Japanese miso — a salty, brownish sauce or paste made from the fermented soybean pulp left behind when soy sauce is brewed. It is sold in cans and jars in most supermarkets under various different names: brown bean paste, brown bean sauce, ground bean paste or bean sauce. The paste can vary from a dark brown to a light golden brown color and may come in the form of a sauce, paste or even whole beans with a bit of sauce around them. The basic bean paste contains just soybeans, water and sugar but seasoned versions contain sugar or chili. If there are whole beans in the paste, these are usually mashed or crushed with the back of a spoon before adding them to sauces. Opened bottles of bean paste will keep in the refrigerator for several months.

Index